TAI CHI CH'UAN
and
SHAMANISM
A Spiritual Union

MICHELINE BOGEY

BALBOA.
PRESS
A DIVISION OF HAY HOUSE

Balboa Press books may be ordered through booksellers or by contacting:

Balboa Press
A Division of Hay House
1663 Liberty Drive
Bloomington, IN 47403
www.balboapress.com
1 (877) 407-4847

Because of the dynamic nature of the Internet, any web addresses or links contained in this book may have changed since publication and may no longer be valid. The views expressed in this work are solely those of the author and do not necessarily reflect the views of the publisher, and the publisher hereby disclaims any responsibility for them.

The author of this book does not dispense medical advice or prescribe the use of any technique as a form of treatment for physical, emotional, or medical problems without the advice of a physician, either directly or indirectly. The intent of the author is only to offer information of a general nature to help you in your quest for emotional and spiritual well-being. In the event you use any of the information in this book for yourself, which is your constitutional right, the author and the publisher assume no responsibility for your actions.

Any people depicted in stock imagery provided by Getty Images are models, and such images are being used for illustrative purposes only. Certain stock imagery © Getty Images.

Print information available on the last page.

ISBN: 978-1-9822-0563-8 (sc)
ISBN: 978-1-9822-0572-0 (e)

Balboa Press rev. date: 06/20/2018

SPIRIT

Prayer to the 4 directions
To the East, I rise into the light
To the West, I face the shadow of darkness
To the North, I stand empowered in my truth
To the South, I embrace the excellence of my soul

Contents

Dedication

To all my Teachers and Students who have given me the best of themselves in most genuine and brilliant ways, I am forever grateful. To my Shaman Spirits and Guided Forces of the Light who nudged me on my Soul's path whenever I felt lost, thank you for showing me the way "Home."

May this book serve the Greater Good of All, and may it inspire you in the remembrance that your Spirit shines through the authentic being of your life and manifests as Divine expression into the Cosmic garden of Love.

Biography

I was fortunate to be born in Paris, France, where the cultural legacy as well as the intellectual scrutiny helped me develop a sense of choice and a rebellious way of thinking. By the time I was 14, I had made up my mind that what I truly wanted was to discover the world. So for the next 12 years, I embarked on a journey which took me from the European dignity of the past, England, Scotland, Holland, Germany, Belgium, Switzerland, Spain, Italy to the richness of folklore of North Africa, to the discovery of the people and rich cultures of Turkey, Iran, Afghanistan and Pakistan which brought me to the mystic land of India and Nepal, where spiritual ancestry is a way of life, to the passionate and colorful hearts of the South American countries, Venezuela, Brazil which led me to the United States where the Native American heritage reawakened ancient memories. Throughout this journey, I have knelt in Cathedrals, kissed holy ground of Mosques, chanted in Buddhist Temples, prayed in Monasteries and sang sacred songs around Medicine Wheels. I have discovered that Spirit is everywhere, in everything and everyone. By opening my consciousness to the multidimensionality of existence, I have been blessed with the remembrance of our capacity to channel and communicate with higher guidance.

Acknowledgment

To Fong Ha, my Taoist Master, husband and father of our children, I am forever grateful for your teachings, and for embodying the compassionate spirit of the Taoist within.

To my cherished daughters who taught me unconditional love, you give my existence a higher reason to be.

To my Shamanic partner Gail and my Spiritual Guide Xubiel, a deep gratitude for guiding me into the realms of Spirit where nothing is as you know it, and into the realms of physical Earth where everything is sacred and pure love.

To my dear friend and sister Daisy, I am grateful to your seeking spirit who brought me to Tai Chi and the Occult Teachings.

To Sylvia Nachlinger, a Shaman of beauty and transformation, thank you for your generous teachings.

To my partner in life Magali, thank you for being an Angel with an illuminated heart. Your loving compassion sustains me in the Light.

I would like to honor and recognize the inspiration of Angeles Arrien and her book "*The Fourfold Way*". I chose the 4 basic powers of the Visionary, Healer, Teacher and Warrior (choosing the Knight) as the structure from which my book was written.

Journey of a Thousand Miles

TAI CHI CHUAN

From the first moment I started to practice Tai Chi Chuan, I had wanted to go back to the spiritual source of these profound teachings. Bridging Eastern and Western philosophies seemed the next natural step in this endeavor, for in my own life experience I have been bridging all cultures, beliefs and dimensions in order to find the spirit within and raise to the reflection of our cosmic consciousness without.

The I belong to Micheline, the incarnated Self. The We belong to Star Bright The Light Weaver- my Higher Self- and the guidance of Ascended Masters, Archangels and Spirit Guides. Therefore we use I or We interchangeably.

It was in the year 2000 that all of this came together. I was teaching Tai Chi Chuan to a group of students. As we started to practice the form, I suddenly felt transported into a much lighter energy and as each movement unfolded, I could hear my inner guidance starting to tell me a story. The journey of a thousand miles was finally revealing its intention and powers, and the forces of Grandmother Earth emerged through each step, with the animals speaking through the journey of Tai Chi, with the heart showing us the dimensions of its power, with the mind constantly reflecting over past and/or future. It was as if a veil had been torn within my inner consciousness, and the glimpses of light perceived through it revealed an extraordinary understanding I had been searching all along. I felt with great excitement the surge of spiritual wisdom of the Tai Chi practice aligning with the cosmic light of life itself, and the realization of my own journey crossed a threshold of awakening. The spiritual union of Tai Chi and Shamanism is, on some level, universal to all of us, for we birth ourselves upon this incredible planet Earth, we grow into the physical, emotional, mental and spiritual being that we are and we ascend into a higher realization of our "Multidimensional Oneness" with each lifetime.

Chapter One

SACRED NUMEROLOGY

Tai Chi Chuan (Tai Qi Quan) uses 8 directions that correspond to the 8 basic trigrams of the I Ching. The I Ching- ancient Chinese "Book of Changes"- is a form of divinatory practice involving 64 hexagrams (patterns of 6 broken and unbroken lines). We added one more direction for, in shamanic understanding, the 9th direction is center and represents Self and the cycle of birth, death and rebirth. The total of 108 postures in the classical form of Tai Chi Chuan adds to the number 9, the end of a cycle and the rebirthing into the next one- and so the 9 directions are created.

Tai Chi Chuan Classical Form includes 3 sections

3 Bodies (vehicles)	3 Manifestations	3 Primary Powers of Creation
Physical	Oneness	Will
Emotional	Duality/Yin yang	Love
Mental	Balance	Wisdom

Section 1 -> 19 moves
Section 2 -> 39 moves
Section 3 -> 49 moves
107 postures +#0 (Wu Ji)= 108 Postures

"Hindus and Buddhists chants use a mala of 108 beads that represents the 108 texts of the *Upanishads*." Stephen Knapp

"The distance between the earth and the sun is approximately 108 times the sun's diameter. The diameter of the sun is about 108 times the earth's diameter. And the distance between the earth and the moon is 108 times the moon's diameter. Could this be the reason the ancient sages considered 108 such a sacred number? If the microcosm (us) mirrors the macrocosm (the solar system), then you could say there are 108 steps between our ordinary human awareness and the divine light at the center of our being. Each time we chant another mantra as our mala beads slip through our fingers, we are taking another step toward our own inner sun." Professor Subhash Kap

"Astronomically, there are 27 constellations in our galaxy, and each one of them has 4 directions, and 27x 4 = 108. In other words, the number 108 covers the whole galaxy. The letter 9 corresponds to Lord Brahma [Creator of universe). Mathematically, the interesting property of 9 is 9x1 = 9 -9x2 = 18 (8+1 = 9) 9x3 = 27 (7+2 = 9) 9x12 = 108 (1+0+8 = 9)." Indian Scriptures

POWER ANIMALS AND ELEMENTALS

Shamanic wisdom teaches that everything is Spirit, and therefore we can communicate with everything. From the Devic Kingdom and the Elemental Kingdom, Nature in all its glory, come the guidance of Power Animals, Plant Allies, Crystal Spirits, Elementals and Directions. We have combined all of these elements to communicate and explore the journey of Tai Chi.

We are aware that different traditions hold different beliefs. We honor these as well and wish to add our personal recognition to the wisdom already realized by the magic of life.

POWER ANIMALS QUALITIES

HORSE

Travel,Power of change, Freedom
#39 #62 #63 #64 #93

COCK

Sexuality, Pride, Vigilance, Resurrection
#76 #77

SNAKE

Rebirth, Initiation, Wisdom, Transmutation
#75 #87 #99

TIGER

Passion, Power, Devotion, Sensuality
#20 #49 #50 #51 #59 #101

FISH

Potential,Awakening,Senses
Adaptation, Independence #22

SPARROW

Awakening,Nobility,
Dignity, Self-worth
#6 #21 #35 #60 #71 #89
#97

DRAGON

Reincarnation,Primordial Power,
Courage, Master of 4 Elements
#17 #34 #47 #56 #88 #104

WHITE CRANE

Longevity, Justice,
Focused Creation
#9 #29 #83

MONKEY

Intelligence,Leadership,
Perception, Resourcefulness
#24 #25 #26 #78 #79 #80

Power animals/ Animal powers

Animals live naturally and spontaneously, doing what they are created to do in their full powers. They never lose their sense of themselves and respond with a fullness of spirit to whatever life presents to them.

Power animals are archetypal energies that are focused into physical reality through the spirit of animals. Each animal holds very unique qualities. These are its gifts, talents, powers. As we call on their power and guidance, they help us develop these qualities in ourselves.

Chapter Two

PHYSICAL BLUEPRINT/SHAMANIC EMBODIMENT
ELEMENTALS   ANIMALS VIRTUES

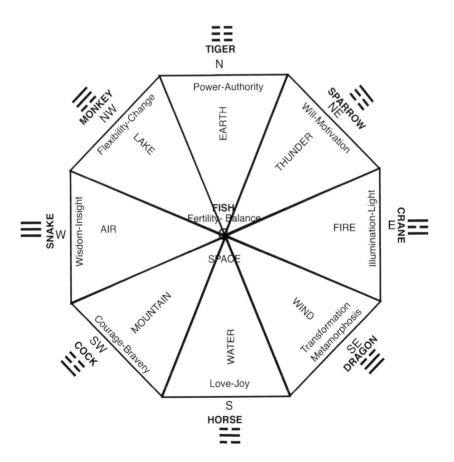

DIRECTIONS- ANIMALS- ELEMENTALS- VIRTUES

North: Tiger – Earth element- Power, Authority

South: Horse – Water element –Love, Joy

East: White Crane - Fire element - Light, Illumination

West: Snake- Air element- Wisdom, Insight

North East: Sparrow- Thunder element- Will, Motivation

North West: Monkey- Lake element- Change, Flexibility

South East: Dragon-Wind Element- Transformation, Metamorphosis

South West: Cock- Mountain Element- Courage, Bravery

Center: Fish- Space Element- Fertility, Balance

The **Bagua** meaning "Eight symbols" are eight trigrams used in Daoist Cosmology to represent the fundamental principles of reality, seen as a range of eight interrelated concepts. Each consists of three lines, each line either "broken" or "unbroken," respectively representing Yin or Yang.

In building the bridge from West to East or East to West, you are now creating the Bagua representing the correlation of Eastern understanding of the directions and elementals with the Western relationship of the directions, the power animals and their virtues.

This Bagua does not reflect the classical Bagua with its directions and elementals. This Bagua represents the physical blueprint of human experience in co-creation with Earth and its natural manifestations.

North represents the anchoring of your power and authority through the Tiger energy into your Physical body-**Earth**

South represents the higher flow of your love and joy through the Horse Power of service and unconditional love into your Emotional body- **Water**

Together, **North and South** connect and join to form *Loving Empowered Authority.*

East represents the awakening of your illuminated soul through flight and freedom of the White Crane into your Etheric body- **Fire**

West represents the truth of your innate wisdom and insight through the metamorphosis of Snake (changing poison into medicine) into your Mental body- **Air**

Together, **East and West** connect and join to form *Illuminated Wisdom with Insight.*

North East represents the higher will of purity with intent through the Sparrow into your Causal body- **Thunder**

South West represents standing up fearlessly through the courage and bravery of the Cock into your Intuitive body. **Mountain**

Together, **North East and South West** connect and join to form *The Bravery of Higher Will.*

North West represents the flexibility of change through the Monkey's movements into your Astral body- **Lake**

South East represents the transformation through the Dragon's metamorphosis into your Atmic body – **Wind**

Together, **North West and South East** connect and join to form *Change as Metamorphosis and Alchemy.*

Center represents the gathering of all elements of fertility, creativity and balance into your Cosmic body- **Space**

**SPIRITUAL BLUEPRINT
ARCHETYPES WITH RIGHT EXPRESSIONS**

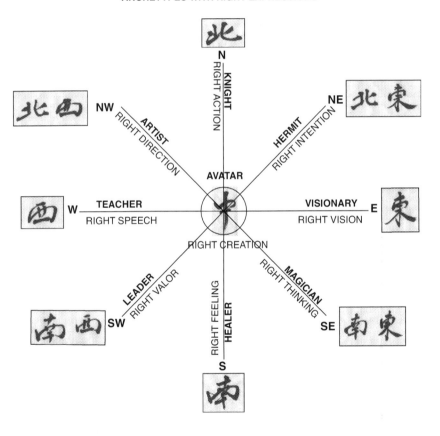

DIRECTIONS- ARCHETYPES – RIGHT EXPRESSIONS

North: Knight Archetype- Right action

South: Healer Archetype- Right feeling

East: Visionary Archetype- Right vision

West: Teacher Archetype- Right speech

North East: Hermit Archetype- Right intention

North West: Artist Archetype- Right direction

South East: Magician Archetype- Right thinking

South West: Leader Archetype- Right valor

Center: Avatar Archetype- Right creation

Spiritual Powers of Archetypes with Right Expressions

SPIRIT

"In Jungian psychology, Archetype is a collectively inherited unconscious idea, pattern of thought, image, etc., universally present in individual psyches."

The Spiritual Powers of Archetypes invoke an authentic resonance of the true nature of the Soul, helping us align to the vibrational frequency of our highest potential. All expressions of Archetypes need to be integrated and self-realized before they can be of service to the Greater Good of All. This Diagram represents the spiritual blueprint of Humanity for Soul growth and Spiritual evolution.

Knight Archetype- Feel Thyself

The true purpose of the Knight Archetype is self-understanding through feelings. The Knight is ruled by the physical world and its survival. The Higher frequency of the Knight is unleashed when the heart's feelings and the understanding of these feelings manifest the "Right Action" serving a greater purpose or greater cause.

Healer Archetype- Heal Thyself

The true purpose of the Healer Archetype is self-healing. The Healer in us is activated by the opening of our love and charity towards All beings, including ourselves and our body. As a result, compassion for self becomes the "Right feeling" that transmutes the disharmonies of our being into a coherent field of loving acceptance. Shamans are some of the oldest healers on Earth.

Visionary Archetype- See Thyself

The true purpose of the Visionary Archetype is self-exploration. The Visionary is inspired to see the "Way" through the revelation of the deeper meaning inherent in all things. The Visionary in us reveals itself through insight and intuition. Tearing the veil of forgetfulness, illusions are shattered, dreams are integrated, and the "Right vision" of consciousness develops into the "bigger picture" of our existence.

Teacher Archetype- Know Thyself

The true purpose of the Teacher Archetype is self-realization. The Teacher Archetype is an Initiator and Communicator. The teacher

Archetype in us develops "Right speech" to communicate stories with discernment, wisdom and inner knowing.

Hermit Archetype- Discover Thyself

The true purpose of the Hermit Archetype is self-discovery. The Hermit Archetype follows the inner quest to find its own light. The Hermit Archetype in us applies the "Right intention" to reveal the truth of one's Soul path.

Artist Archetype- Imagine Thyself

The true purpose of the Artist Archetype is self-expression. The Artist Archetype unlocks the original creative power from within. The Artist Archetype in us seeks enchantment in the "right direction" by imagining and creating endless possibilities of beauty, inspiration and grace.

Magician Archetype- Transform Thyself

The true purpose of the Magician Archetype is self-transformation. The Magician Archetype creates sacred spaces where metamorphosis occurs. The Magician Archetype in us trusts the intuition as "Right thinking" for the purpose of change and transformation.

Leader Archetype- Rule Thyself

The true purpose of the Leader Archetype is self-governing. The Leader Archetype takes responsibility for the enfoldment of its destiny. The Leader Archetype in us empowers its authority with "Right valor" to guide and manifest its latent potential.

Avatar Archetype- Create Thyself

The true purpose of the Avatar Archetype is self-creation. The Avatar-meaning to cross over- Archetype anchors Spirit into Matter. The Avatar Archetype in us incarnates its divinity with "Right creation" to embody unconditional love and wisdom in action.

CALLING OF THE DIRECTIONS

East: When you stand in the East, you face the rising sun, the light of illumination of the yang energies that are rising within all things, the new beginnings. Your awareness is focused towards vision and the energy of the visionary that is to be awakened within. You are receiving the light of consciousness, the fire element, to help you fuel your visions and your dreams, to well up from within your creative life force. You are activating your spiritual awakening.

South: When you stand in the South, the power of love envelops you into its energy of hope and unconditional acceptance. Loving-kindness brings the healer within you, allowing you to surrender to the compassion of your true emotional nature. As you embrace all beings as yourself, all possibilities are created, and your oneness with the universe is complete. You are activating your emotional awakening.

West: When you stand in the West, facing the setting sun, you call in the energies of wisdom and you awaken the teacher within. You are receiving the mindful teachings of the air element, bringing clarity of intention within as you internalize and experience the lessons of the knowledge of mind/ heart. You are centering the mental self into a place of wisdom.

North: When you stand in the North, the North Star guides your steps with unflinching determination, to manifest the creator into the created, the journey of spirit into matter. The Earth calls the Knight in you, and with the courage and willpower to focus your intent, you make the dream a reality.

Center: All of the energies of the 8 directions then converge toward the Center of the wheel, and the 9th direction is created. Your enlightened consciousness is then capable of focusing this pure frequency of light, love, wisdom and truth into the present, where the self in matter and the Higher Self in Spirit are one, and the cycle of co-creation fulfills its sacred purpose.

Throughout the practice of Tai Chi Chuan, you will turn toward the 8 directions. Under the influence of the number 8, infinity will be recreated and all the possibilities within explored.

From the **East,** under the energy of the **Crane,** you awaken the visionary and the light of spirit.

From the **South,** under the energy of the **Horse,** you acknowledge the healer and the light of love.

From the **West,** under the energy of the **Snake,** you recall the teacher and the light of wisdom.

From the **North**, under the energy of the **Tiger,** you embody the warrior and the light of power.

Then you rotate toward the 4 complementary directions where the energies fuse to become the Oneness of Self.

From the **South East,** under the energy of the **Dragon,** you awaken the Magician and the light of transformation where you become the awakened Visionary and magical Healer.

From the **South West,** under the energy of the **Cock,** you direct the Leader with valor and you become the wise Leader and guided Healer.

From the **North West,** under the energy of the **Monkey,** you manifest the Artist with change and flexibility and you become the inspired Warrior and empowered Teacher.

From the **North East,** under the energy of the **Sparrow,** you create the Hermit and the light of will, and you become the insightful Warrior and Visionary Hermit.

From the **Center,** under the energy of the **Fish,** you awaken the Avatar standing with all its manifested gifts as Creator.

In the physical world of duality of this Earth plane, you will practice your Tai Chi Chuan on both right and left sides, which will bring these complementary and polarized energies into balance within your 4 bodies.

POWER WHEEL

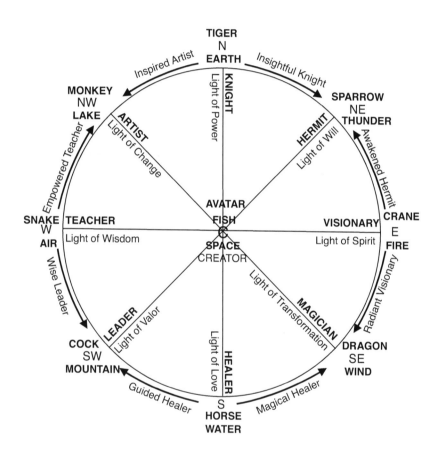

The Power Wheel represents the "Medicine Wheel" of your potential, possibilities and probabilities. As you move through your Tai Chi practice and fuse with the directions [Path], elementals [Breath] and animals [Qi], the Archetypal Powers of your spiritual journey unfold. At the start of your practice, the raw elements of your energies reflect the imbalances of your mental, emotional and physical selves.

As you open unto the power of your practice, the centering and balancing of your energy anchor your four bodies to co-create a physical journey that is harmonious, flowing and awakened.

As you choose with intent the direction of your practice, the portals and powers of that direction will influence the outcome of your journey.

Chapter Three

SECTION 1 / SELF

第一節 Throughout the section 1, you will find yourself under the influence of the number 1, the self, the individual consciousness. In an evolved level, the self becomes the Higher Self, the Divine Self, without separation from its original creation. As you are born upon this planet Earth, you experience the self into matter with learning and feelings attached to the emotional body. As you grow into your physical self, the feelings become stronger for the lessons to be learned and the journey of stepping into the embodiment of your physical life begins. How do you stand as Homo Erectus? How do you shift your weight from left to right to balance the polarity of your physical nature? How do you breathe in your world and breathe out your individual self so you are constantly regenerating your act of creation with All and Everything? How do you harmonize your body physical with your Earth matter? These considerations will be explored in Section 1.

Section 1 includes 19 moves. 1+9=10=1

For the purpose of this book, we will start the Tai Chi journey facing East.

O- Wu Ji Stance / Creation

Wu Ji literally means ultimate, boundless, infinite. 0 encompasses the energy of the void, the womb of creation, the all knowing, the circle, the circle of life, the circular time versus linear time, the time that goes into infinity, forward and backward, the Quantum time. When you stand at the center of the circle, you see your future, you see your now, you see your past, there is no end to what you can direct forward, there is no end to what comes behind, for as the earth is a circle, time follows the planetary circle and what seems to be a straight line will become a circle at some point. The line to the front toward the future, the line to the back toward the past will join, and when you stand at the center of your circle, you have a view of the now, with the past, the present and the future into one. There you stand, in the wholeness of your being, at one with the energies of spirit and matter, uniting the Cosmic will with the human will to manifest the Greater Self.

1- Tai Chi Commencement / Oneness

You stand in the glory of your I Am presence, you stand between Heaven and Earth, between the illumination of your spirit and the manifestation of your powers upon the Earth plane. You stand and become One with Heaven and Earth, with all that is, with what is above and what is below, you stand in the knowing of who you are. You stand in the stillness, in the void, feeling the beginning of motion, movement and creation. In that stillness, you take a moment to align your vibrations with the Higher Self, so that the Tai Chi-Supreme Ultimate- consciousness of your Spirit may be allowed to be fully embodied. In the stillness, you also align your energy rhythms with the flow of the Earth rhythms, allowing the powers of matter to build up in your physical body, so that the sacred vessel that is the body may be able to manifest into your life your dreams, your visions, your cosmic purpose. So you stand fully present, fully aware, becoming the creator and the created simultaneously, your Oneness of Spirit manifested in the Oneness of your individualized uniqueness. As movement stirs within you, you allow these energies to move your body into the commencement of your journey and you create the ball of Qi-energy ball- that you will carry on your path of discovery and self-knowledge.

2- Ward-Off / Duality

You step into your "Ward-Off" and there you step into the energy of 2, duality where the Yin and Yang begin to manifest. Within the void, out of the One, the movement of Yin and Yang has been created. Within the void exists the creation of all that is, and as you become one with it, you feel and sense your circle, you align your centers and you step into your "Ward-Off," warding off an aspect of your self. You "Ward-Off" the beginning of the journey, for you have come from the Oneness into the duality of Yin and Yang. Until you can stand in the center of your polarity, you will be warding off one or the other, trying to understand and balance the female and the male energies within, your empowerment and the absence of it, the fear and the love. This is the "Ward Off" that happens consciously and unconsciously, as you stand as the warrior ready to struggle and battle in the journey of your life.

3- Double Ward-Off / Sacred Geometry

You bring a double energy to the ward off, for you are becoming stronger and denser. You are manifesting yourself in a stronger way for you are now under the influence of the number 3. The energy of 3 represents the Divine unity expressed into the physical manifestation of matter through the duality of Yin and Yang. It is the sacred geometry of the Pyramids, where the Cosmic Will of Divine Source expresses itself into matter and where the wisdom of this transformation is imprinted, sculpted into the stones. With the power of 3, you encounter the beginning of challenges that allow you to grow, challenges that you need to face on the particular path that you have chosen in this present lifetime, helping you rediscover who you are. You "Double Ward Off," you double the energies, feeling the need to stand strong in the face of adversity or in the face of the unknown.

4- Roll Back / Overview

You give space to yourself by yielding to the pressure, by rolling back. You "Roll Back" physically, emotionally, mentally, you have an opportunity to look behind, already having an overview of the past, or at least a good look at what you brought with you. You give yourself the opportunity to yield and to place yourself in a feminine, non-aggressive posture where you recoil, where you take that knowledge in, where you decide the next step forward. You find yourself now under the vibrational influence of the number 4, the energy of matter, the earth, the 4 directions, the 4 seasons, the 4 bodies, the Great Mother, pure Yin energy as the Earth itself, nurturing and sustaining your physical life. "As you Roll Back," you take a moment to observe where you came from and where you are going. You call upon the wisdom of the feminine, the ability to trust the intuition within, to recognize the truth of where you stand and the direction to follow.

5- Press / Limitations

As you move into the "Press," you press against the energy that seems to be pressing against you. You want to extend your energy, you want to experience, and in the experience sometimes you feel uptight, pressed upon and you want to expand. You are under the energy of 5, the energy of self-reliance, represented by the 5 fingers that reach out into the world, the 5 toes that allow you to walk your path as a self-reliant individual. In order to stand into your self-reliance, there is a need to explore and experience the self beyond the known, beyond the safe structure already built. You press against the patterns already established within you, to prove to the self that you hold within the capacity as well as the courage to confront the unknown, with the certainty of being able to face the challenges to come. You rely upon the self and you press against your limitations.

6- Push / Union

In the energy of the "Push", you gather your momentum to push forward, to continue to push through the denser energies that you have encountered since the beginning of your journey. You find yourself in the energy of the number 6, the union of Spirit into matter represented by the sacred symbol of the cross, the vertical line of spiritual energy cutting through the horizontal line of material energy, forming the highest consciousness of Love into the heart of humankind. With the union of 6, the Spirit that you are is capable of bringing a whole new and different consciousness into your being, and you begin to feel a stir of awakening within. With the energy of Spirit, the self starts to lift into a higher level of love and understanding.

While you are doing these 5 movements "Ward Off, Double Ward Off, Roll Back, Press and Push," you enter once again into the energy of self reliance, confronted with what you are facing, starting to build your self reliance at the beginning of your journey. This journey is infinite; it has neither beginning nor end. However, it starts at the moment your consciousness is present in the journey. This energy of 5 helps you push, stand and face the adversity, the challenges and the lessons that you have chosen in this present time. These energies combined are called "Grasping the Sparrow's Tail."

"Grasping the Sparrow's Tail." What are you grasping at? You are grasping at the dignity and the nobility that the sparrow represents. The sparrow was the bird present in the time of the crucifixion, in time of suffering, and it holds an energy of survival that is unparalleled. Its nobility and endurance bring the will forward, the will to live, the willingness to bring forth the dignity of life within the self. When you "Grasp the Sparrow's Tail," you are grasping at an aspect of dignity

and willpower that reside within and which you do not want to let go of, for if you let go of it, you might get lost upon a different path, into a different energy. "Grasping the Sparrow's Tail" is uniting the dignity and the will to become who you are in all your powers, with strength and endurance, with nobility of action and thought, with dignity of Spirit. You started with the vibration of 2 and you end with the vibration of 6, while performing "Grasping the Sparrow's Tail," from duality to unity, a representation of your Spirit into your journey of life. It is a moment in time for you to remember to stand and to bring forth the will, to dignify your self and to live your life in the truth of your being.

7- Single Whip / Past Karma

As you catch a breath of that truth, you then want to assert it, spread it across, and as you do so, you whip. You whip your energy outward, you whip it in an intent and action that are Yang, for you have gathered throughout the first 6 movements the beginning of your own leadership and powers. You understand and feel the pressure and the challenges facing you. You have grasped an aspect of the Divine Spirit that you are, and now you bring it forth physically in a positive, concrete and Yang energy, so you "Single Whip." You whip it through you, you whip it through the energies around you, you assert it into your life. You are under the influence of the number 7, often called the number of karma. Karma represents all the actions that you have ever taken and their repercussions. You are faced with the Law of Cause and Effect and with this first round of "Single Whip," you meet the lessons that you brought with you from the past, the needed completion of your personal story.

8- Lift Hands and Step Up / Self-Knowledge

As you "Lift Hands and Step Up," you gather energy from the Earth and you lift your hands toward the Heavens. It is a gesture of taking what is given to you and opening to receive what is coming to you. You step up into a different awareness, choosing to stand into the initiation of a whole new awakening, albeit still fragile. You lift your hands to receive the guidance from above, to gather the energies from below, and you step up into this transformed awareness with renewed hope. You are feeling the influence of the number 8 representing infinite motion throughout the universe, changes bringing growth in multitudes of ways. As you open to receive these revitalized energies, you release the resistance and fear and you allow change to open a window of your soul. Through your willingness to change, you meet the self in a new light and you welcome the process of transformation as the next step towards self-knowledge.

9- White Crane Spreads its Wings / Inner Knowing

The crane is a symbol of justice, of longevity, of creation. It is a symbol that represents an ancient wisdom that has been with you at all times and is about to be recovered. In the longevity of the crane, there is a wisdom of ancient knowledge, of past life experiences, for in circular time, you reach backward into the past and you reach forward into the future, and you find your past lives and your future possibilities. The crane allows you for a moment to reopen the memory of the past as well as extending your recognition into the future. The crane is symbolic of being a spiritual expression of the Self, a feminine energy, for it is a bird of the waters even though it flies, and as it flies it brings spirit into the feminine energy of your Yin and Yang. The white symbolizes purity and as you become the White Crane and spread your wings, you start to open to a pure, untouched, sincere and true quality in you. You open to the essence of who you are, to the truth of your Spirit. You bring forth the memory of the Spirit that you are by standing in the White Crane and spreading your wings. You stand in a place and time where you can reach beyond space and time, where you are, for one moment, all that you have ever been in the Spirit world, in your feminine energy, in all that you can bring back from intuition, from inner knowing. It is a celebration of rebirth, of existence, of your creative resources and how to manifest it as you spread your wings. The crane has a focus, and it is in holding the proper focus of your life that you will be able to bring forth the higher purpose of the journey that you have chosen. As you gather the dignity and the will to survive, as you extend yourself into your greater potential, you stand in the magnificence of the White Crane and its energy. As you spread this energy, you reach forward and back, future and past gathering the knowledge into the present, into the now. With a pure heart, with a pure focus and intent, as white as the white crane, you then walk the path of your destiny.

The number 9 is the number of rebirthing. You have completed a cycle, the first of many cycles that you will complete in many lifetimes. As you stand in that space, you hold yourself in the Essence of Spirit, the awareness of purity and light. You rebirth yourself anew, encompassing all, spreading your wings towards the Heavens, towards the Earth into the qualities, gifts and talents that you are now rediscovering within.

10- Brush Knee and Step Forward (L) / Outer Expression

As you start again your journey, you "Brush Knee and Step Forward." You find yourself stepping upon your path, you and the universe, you and your journey, for you are now under the influence of the number 10, the self with the circle of universal energy, the circle of life and death, the circle of all possibilities. It is a moment where you are once again under the vibration of 0, the circle that holds the entirety within. It is that energy of wholeness that is gathered unto the self in order to brush whatever is in front of you, removing it out of the way in a fully integrated action and emotion. You step forward, feeling the support of the universe reflecting itself unto you with a renewed energy. As you do this, you focus in a direction, you give yourself an intention and you take action. This is a Yang energy that is coming in, after gathering the Yin energies from the crane. The Oneness of your Spirit with the universal cycle is recognized, honored and followed.

11- Play the Lute / Song of Spirit

As you step forward into "Play the Lute," there is a moment of recoil, where you need to center and assert that you are on the right path for yourself, and you enter the resonance of the number 11. The Lute is an old string instrument, similar to the guitar, from the same family. When you "Play the Lute," you play an inner music, centering the self where you can hear your inner voice, the voice of the Soul, telling you if you are on the right path, guiding you with its song and its melody. The lute holds 6 to 13 strings, 6 the base of spirit energy to 13, the death and rebirth energy, so it is between these energies that you find once again, the renewal and realignment of yourself. You "Play the Lute" and the magic of these celestial sounds touches your spirit, and your heart is awakened once again to follow its calling, to trust its journey. You now hold the energy of the number 11, you and the guided song of your spirit, you the self with the greater Self, standing side by side, standing one into another, playing the Soul song for the personality that you are and the melody that you resonate at, helping you walk your path in the right direction. That energy of double one, free will standing side by side with choice, creates the willpower necessary to continue the guided journey of Divine existence.

12- Brush Knee and Step Forward (L)/

13- Brush Knee and Step Forward (R)/

14- Brush Knee and Step Forward (L)/ Awakening the Warrior Within

As you step into the number 12, you are going to "Brush Knee and Step Forward" three times, 12, 13, and 14, because you are going to brush, once again, whatever you felt was holding you back, whatever doubts or uncertainties you had at this moment in your life, and you are going to step forward, left, right, left, balancing your Yin and Yang, aware of each step. The number three is the number of energy, the sacred geometry of the pyramid, the triangle, the communion of 1 and 2 together, of the Divine Self and the human self, the self and duality, so that you can birth the will of your soul. It is the energy of Spirit, pushing you, helping you forward. It is the warrior within awakening to its powers of intention, decisions and will, wanting to carry forth its purpose. In these steps, you are merging with the vibrations of 13 and 14. The self finds that this duality inspires a new action fueled with the power of 3 in 13, a direction with intent, wanting to manifest in the energy of 4 as 14.

These steps represent the willingness to keep going, to go forward no matter what, the indomitable spirit in action, a conscious decision of choice and free will generating a leap forward in faith and a joyful recognition of one's own powers.

15- Play the Lute / Call of Spirit

Every time you make a move forward, every time you gather energy and step forward in your life, there is a need for reassessing the path that you have chosen, there is a need to center the self and join with the Higher Self. As you "Play the Lute" for the second time, you call once again upon your Soul song and the guidance of the Celestial Realms is able to let you hear the wisdom of your decisions, able to let you feel the positive vibrations permeating your body like waves of light, the melody of pure energy. It is with the power of 5, the power of self-reliance that you trust this guidance, willing to take responsibility for going forward, for the choices that you make. As you empower the self, you recognize that you have what is needed to succeed, perceiving the call of Spirit and trusting that inner voice's guidance that accompanies you at all times. You listen intently to the inner music of the Soul which tremors as true vibrations felt in your heart. This is the inner knowing you rely upon to continue your journey, playing the melody of your life upon the strings of your experiences.

16- Brush Knee and Step Forward (L) / Path of Choice

Coming from this place of inner knowing, you "Brush Knee and Step Forward" one more time, needing that confirmation unto the self. You brush the last residues of past doubts, the uncertainties that the mind bring forth in its energy of duality. You step forward into the future that comes around and joins with the past. The renewal of the commitment to your Cosmic journey is felt, acknowledged and accepted. At that moment, you are fully supported by the energy of 16, sustained by the 6 of Spirit uniting with the one, the unique individual that you are. You understand, on some level, that you cannot err on your path. You can only experience and grow through your choices, sometimes repeating the same occurrences in order to fully grasp the gold of the journey's wisdom, just like you repeat "Brush Knee and Step Forward" as many times as necessary in order to complete the karmic cycle you have entered into long ago.

17- Dragon Step Forward, Parry and Punch / Power of Transformation

As you step into the vibration of 17, you parry and punch. You reach a place of confrontation, challenge, karma (7), the energies of the causes that you have made in the past, the effects that you face in the present and the waves that ripple into the future. As you find yourself facing this moment, you need the Yang energy of punch and power in order to break through the quagmire of past beliefs and feelings that do not serve you anymore. It is with that consciousness that you "Step Forward, Parry and Punch," that you block energies that are coming at you. You deflect these feelings that are rising within the self as you realize that they are not for your greater good. You punch with the will power and the focus intent that you have gathered until now and the punch becomes the symbol of action expressed in the physical realm. It represents the actions that you take in your life, for you are not afraid to face your fears, you are not afraid to take action, following the call of your Spirit. You are within the vibration of the dragon. The dragon is created from many different animals, and therefore holds the energies of all of them. The dragon represents all of the lives that you have ever lived into one moment in time, and when you step with the dragon step, you have the opportunity to transform the past and create the future into an empowered present. The power of transformation that the dragon brings will help you transmute in a whole new light the karmic experiences that you have created for yourself.

18- Withdraw and Push / Centering Within

As you carry yourself into the number 18, you "Withdraw and Push." Some would say you close the energy. After acknowledging where you stand and taking action, you need to set yourself in an objective place where you can realize what has been done and the rippling effects of your actions, feeling the reactions that come with it. Therefore, you withdraw and you bring the energy within. After the Yang of action, you take the energy of Yin and you withdraw to center within, to recognize where you stand in that new consciousness, to gather what you have learned and what you have done, acknowledging full responsibility as you push forward. You recognize that, no matter what, you continue and your ability to respond is there in your push, in your willingness to confront the obstacles, your inner fears and doubts. You receive the energy of change from the number 8 with gratitude for being able to accept, forgive and let go of past actions, and with change always comes growth and the lessons to be learned bring you closer to the truth of your essential self.

19- Cross Hands / Balance

As you make a turn into the number 19, you step into your "Cross Hands." When you join your hands, or when you join your wrists in physical terms of the movement, you join the Yin and Yang, the perfect harmony into a perfect balance. At that moment, you stand in the Buddha's land, you stand in the awareness of the Christ consciousness, you "Cross Hands" and you are one within the duality, you are one with all that surrounds you, you form the circle once again, you have joined the past and future lines together into the eternal cycle of infinity. You hit the number 19, and you, the self, stand into the completion of a cycle and the rebirthing of another. You have experienced the self from many angles, with many feelings and realizations, from 0 to 19, and you now ready yourself to step into the next cycle of growth, the cycle of 2, the duality that influences everything you do and everything you think.

As you Cross Hands and have come a full cycle, you face the East again, the Light guiding you, the Spirit within facing the inner light one more time.

SECTION 2/ DUALITY

 Under the energy of section2, duality comes into full force. It involves the duality of all your beliefs. The foundation upon which you built the image of self is being shattered by the emotional experiences that now give a whole different view and understanding of what your life is about and how you feel about it.
The opposite and complementary forces of everything created upon this plane come into your reality as you now experience

your Yin and Yang through the emotional body, ready to experience the teachings of duality.

In order to create the energy of 2, the Divine Oneness had to split to manifest the opposites existing into the core of all unity, just as the light splits itself into 7 rays in order to manifest the colors already inherent in the light. Consequently, the journey begins from unity to multidimensional beingness, from cellular consciousness to its holographic response into cosmic consciousness, from the individual to the group. After standing in the oneness of your being, you accept to encounter duality once again in order to experience, accept and balance your feelings and emotions.

Section 2 progresses with the opening of your Heart Field. How do you reconcile your duality from fear to love, from retreat to courage, from the willfulness to manifest to the willingness to love?

These considerations will be explored in Section 2.

Section 2 includes 39 moves. 3+9=12=1 self+ 2 duality

20- Embrace Tiger and Return to the Mountain / Embracing your Fears

You step into the energy of 20, the duality and the universe standing side by side, the duality of Yin and Yang and the void, the energy of infinite possibilities. As you do so, you "Embrace Tiger and Return to the Mountain." The tiger will always help you face your fears, deep fears from long ago, fear of the unknown, fear of the outside world, because now you are not into your oneness, but you are into the duality of your world. You have separated yourself, and in this separation, you fear what is outside your self, and sometimes you fear what is inside the self as well. As you stand and embrace the tiger, you agree to recognize and acknowledge holding your fears within. With that recognition, you are willing to change, heal, and transcend those fears, and you return to the mountain, the path of your life that you climb with every experience, every sorrow and every pleasure. Each time you turn around, you find yourself a little bit higher up on the mountain, with a new perspective, a new understanding, for you now stand with the awareness of self and the world around you, the self between Heaven and Earth, the self and the path that you are creating, even though it might seem strange or foreign to you at this stage.

21- Grasp the Sparrow's Tail / Power of the Will

This "Grasp the Sparrow's Tail" happens in a diagonal direction, for there is a need now to recollect the self, to bring the will forward and the dignity you hold within in order to deal with those fears and this duality of the self. You stand in a different direction and because of it you perceive a different view that shows you that without your will to survive, without the nobility and endurance of your quest, you could not face the duality of your self, you could not face your fears. Standing in the diagonal direction, you align yourself with the Lei lines of the Earth, the energy lines of power of the Earth, bringing a greater force to your determination to challenge the obstacles to come. Under the energy of 21, the duality within the self, you are learning to find your allies in the Devic Kingdom, the Devas and Spirits of Nature, for you realize that you are not alone on that journey. It is you with the Divine will, it is you with your Cosmic purpose, it is you on your Earthy journey. It is you standing with all of creation.

22- Bagua Fish / Emotional Self

The Bagua represents the Eight Trigrams of the I Ching. These trigrams are used to classify all the phenomena of the universe into 8 categories. Here the fish comes into life. The fish dwells in the water, the element of the emotions, the astral realm. The "Bagua Fish" brings the awareness to the emotional body and its ability to astral travel and discover new aspects of the self. Within the emotional body are held infinite possibilities, available experiences of all phenomena bringing learning and growth. You now stand in the energy of 22, a 4 squared, for these energies are squared, taking you to the number 8, the 8 directions of the "Bagua Fish." The number 8 holds the energies of infinity and eternity, and here in the "Bagua Fish" you find infinity of emotions coming to the surface of your consciousness as you walk the path of duality, the duality of the self with the universe, the duality of the self with the emotional self. The "Bagua Fish" forms the octahedron, the 8 directions of going around and looking within to recognize where you stand emotionally. Working with the "Bagua Fish" is learning to swim in the waters of your life, in the ebb and flux of your emotions. It is learning to recognize, balance and accept all your emotions, to remember their impact and to learn their lessons.

23- Fist Under Elbow / Alignment

You step into a place where you need to align your Yang energy. This movement helps you align the fist, the elbow, the knee and the foot, and in this alignment the awareness says "if there is a need to fight, to protect or to take any actions from all those emotions that are floating to the surface, we are ready". Through the alignment of your whole being, you shift your center line from a place of duality to a place of center, on one foot, for there is a need to recollect the emotional aspects of the self that are being examined and bring them into an alignment, a unity, a single direction. So "Fist Under Elbow" directs all these energies into a Yang action with the warrior coming through, as well as recoiling into a Yin posture of preparation and gathering the knowledge from a different perspective. You are under the influence of the 2 and 3, for the duality that you experience has now created itself into a force and a direction with intent, just like an arrow aimed at a certain target. You are stretching the bow of your emotions and readying yourself to release the arrow of your intent into the next stage of growth, experiencing the karmic law of cause and effect through the emotional self.

24- Step Back and Repulse Monkey (L)/

25- Step Back and Repulse Monkey (R)/

26- Step Back and Repulse Monkey (L)/
Contemplation

As you choose the Yin energy, you "Step Back and Repulse Monkey" and you repeat these 3 times. Monkey is an animal of great flexibility and agility. Monkey does not stay in one place for very long. It is considered a symbol of the mind that is very active and often jumps from one thought to another in a very quick fashion. That is why you repulse monkey, for you realize that the mind is taking you to too many places, as you try to gather the emotional self. You step back and give yourself the space to center, to subdue the monkey mind in order to bring more clarity. You step back 3 times, for that energy multiplied gives you a space of stillness to abide into. As you step back, you step into a place within where you gather your powers and your emotions, where you look at the meanders of the mind and assess what will be the next direction to follow. You step back into yourself in a place of contemplation within, so that the emotional self will be able to express itself without limitations, without denial, without resistance. The great activity of the monkey becomes a true power when used with the right intent, for it generates motivation and a lot of hope in the direction you intend to go. Under these influences, there is a great deal of power that is gathered within. It is a time when you truly observe and realize how the mind triggers the emotional self into certain responses, how it can control, limit or deny altogether the emotions' messages. As you step back in order to step out of the whirlwind of the monkey mind, you are able to recognize the designs and the callings of the heart.

27- Diagonal Flying / Karmic Wheel

From a place of centered heart, you fly into a new direction. The heart and its intent are realigned, the vision is clearer, the emotional self is now ready to step into a whole new vibration and to fly with new wings. You find yourself under the influence of the number 7, and the duality that you carry is now fully revealed through the emotional karma you have embraced since your birthing upon this plane. It is a time to take responsibility for becoming the adult, for choosing what emotions and beliefs' systems belong to you and those that do not. You discover, at this point in time, that many of your pains and emotional baggage are attached to the karmic family wheel you entered and grew up with. It is time to fly with your own wings, recognizing the powers and strength you behold. In your willingness to let go of the karmic family past, you choose to create a new you that will help change the old patterns and the old sufferings. In "Diagonal Flying" you choose to fly in a whole new light, lifted with a renewed sense of self, gliding on the energy of hope and discovery, flying ever closer to your spiritual truth.

28- Lift Hands and Step Up / Spirit Guidance

As you step into #28, your consciousness lifts once again towards the Heaven and grounds itself into the Earth. You pull the energy from above to be spiritually guided into your journey of karmic resolution. After centering the mind and recognizing the pull of the past, you align yourself between Heaven and Earth, and with it you align the mind, the heart and the intention in order to hear the call of your Soul. You "Lift Hands and Step Up," calling force the courage and commitment to be all that you are, to continue to search and to grow with the changes. You are now under the energies of #8, movement of infinite changes, opening you to a greater sense of self, forever exploring the limitless possibilities of evolution through the emotional body. However, duality is still at work and the need to center the self into a place of clarity as well as emotional strength is greater than before, and through the duality of the mind as well as the duality of the heart, you are coming closer to your spiritual state of being. You Lift Hands to receive guidance from your inner Soul, to follow the truth of Spirit, and you Step Up into the upcoming challenges of the unknown.

29- White Crane Spreads its Wings / Self-Realization

As you become the white crane again, you contemplate the longevity of your life, the eternal time-space continuum of your existence. You want to spread your wings even further, to explore the purity of heart and mind together, that energy that holds no doubt. The mind, when influenced by duality, creates doubt and confusion in the heart as well as in the actions taken. You stand in "White Crane Spreads its Wings", centering the mind to reflect a clarity of intent, surrendering the knowing of the heart to the deeper truth of your being, merging the two into a sense of absolute contentment, a blissful realization, where duality dissolves into the Oneness of the Higher Self. You spread your wings, for you need to explore and extend this new awakening into your life, to reassert as well as recognize the essence of who you are. You are under the influence of 2 and 9, the duality that comes to completion, for you have gone through a great array of feelings, emotions and thoughts that created conflicts and doubts, challenges and sometimes sorrow in mind and heart. You are now ready to complete that cycle and focus the mind into a purity of intent where duality disappears into the clear consciousness of the "White Crane Spreads its Wings'" stance, where you are mentally and emotionally motivated to act honestly and truthfully upon the next page of the book of your life.

30- Brush Knee and Step Forward (L) / Path of Recognition

Every time you align yourself into a place of purity, there is a need to step forward, to brush the doubts and confusion created by the mind and to advance on the path of recognition. You are stepping into the energy of 30, 3 and 0 aligned with each other. The power and the intention directed with the will are multiplied by the energy of the circle, the 0, the universal atom and molecule held in the memory of the DNA, the memory of your past. There is an opening of the consciousness at 30, for you have cleared some of the confusion of the scattered mind and you have had an emotional realization of Self. This energy pushes you forward, urging you into a deeper exploration of yourself on your Cosmic path through the duality held within the perspective of your personality. You ask yourself "Who am I? What is it that I am here to learn, to accomplish, to manifest? What is my higher purpose, what is it that only I can create through the duality of this world?" With this inquiry, you "Brush Knee and Step Forward" with a renewed intention and awareness.

31- Needle at Sea Bottom / Ocean of Compassion

You find yourself stepping into "Needle at Sea Bottom," the bottom of the emotional sea that you hold within. All the emotions that you ever felt exist in that place, and you want to find the needle. This needle, like a laser beam focused in its intent, points you to the wounds, the core essence of your emotional body where past emotional hurts and pains have not yet been healed. You want to find that specific energy that will help you emerge out to sea, coming to the surface where you can find a peaceful heart. Under 31, the 1 of self finds itself challenged with the energy of duality of mind and emotions. In between the two, there is a central axis, a place that harmonizes duality. You search for the needle, digging within the emotional self to find that balance, that center core, that space within where duality disappears into Oneness, where pain and sufferings melt into an ocean of compassion and understanding. In this bottomless emotional state, you realize that your mind tries to control the decisions that you make, but the truth and certainty of your heart help you navigate the sea of your experiences. At the core of the sea bottom, in the depths of loving kindness, exists a voice that always reconnects you with the greater potential of your existence. With the power of 3, you cross that threshold, you change your karma on this physical Earth, you transform the emotional self and its entrenched patterns into a springboard of enthusiasm and renewed mission, anchoring your magic "I Am presence" in the doing. The doubts and uncertainties of the mind are drowned into the call of your soul, and from the depths of your heart surge the hope and willpower necessary to continue forward.

32- Fan Through Back / Determination

Having had the courage to dig into the depths of your emotions, you are coming out of it with strength and a backbone that allows you to step forward, to stand into your capability and face any challenges. You spread your "Fan Through Back," the fan representing the ability to express the potency of your emotions, the courage to face your pain, the willingness to heal the heart. That energy runs through your back, becoming the axle of your strength and determination and spreading into your emotional self, just like the axle of the fan holds and helps spread the fan altogether. This is a Yang movement, which uses the power of 3 to push through the resistance of duality. In that moment, there is no more holding back. The awareness of your emotional realization is fueled with the energy of determination, coming from the depths of feelings into the light of manifestation. You center yourself in a place of power, you make a decision to go forward and to open the fan of all dimensions within the emotional self, merging and aligning the intention of the mind with the certainty of the heart.

33- Turn Around and Whip Punch / Facing your Shadow

As you step into the energy of #33, you Turn Around and Whip Punch. Because you are spreading your consciousness and your ability to challenge whatever it is that is coming towards you, you realize that you have to "Turn Around and Whip Punch." Turning around means that you are capable of looking back, looking back at your shadow. In your shadow, you carry the emotional baggage that you have not been able to forgive and truly let go. Until there is an understanding and forgiveness of these experiences, you will continue to carry the shadow aspect of these emotions, resurfacing from time to time. As you have allowed yourself to come up from the depth of the emotional core of your being, embracing your strengths and your power and being willing to face your challenges, you now have to turn back, recognize your feelings and take action. Whip punch is taking that action by stepping into the shadow of your emotional self, turning around and facing old patterns that have been repressed, denied and never healed. In turning around, you face the shadow of your self that is always with you, that holds your fears, your uncertainties and the unresolved issues of your heart. With the energy of 33, your power is squared, and in order to face and transform your present experiences, you have to face your unresolved emotional past and be willing to forgive and complete this part of the journey.

34- Dragon Step Forward, Parry and Punch / Cause and Effect

In order to face your past, you "Dragon Step Forward, Parry and Punch." Once again, you step into all the aspects of who you are in the energy of the Dragon, facing past and future in that present realization of your emotional growth. Because the Dragon holds the qualities of all the animal kingdom, and is created from different parts of animals, it symbolizes all of your lifetimes, so the emotional issues facing you are coming from a distant past as well as present time, and are resurfacing in order to be healed and transformed. You step into that energy, being willing to see with the eyes of the Dragon and look at all angles, all dimensions, to become finally aware of the Karmic Law of Cause and Effect brought about by your recognition of emotional patterns, deeply embedded into the unconscious, coming to the surface in order to bring completion and freedom to the heart. For like the Dragon, your emotional Self is created from all that you have ever felt, from the deepest sorrow to the greatest love, and each one of these feelings will need to be understood, accepted, realized and transcended into pure love. If not resolved, these emotional issues will continue to influence your present choices from a wounded place and lack of forgiveness. Here in the energy of 34, your emotional structure manifests in all its powers as well as in all its unresolved energies, and the choice you make at this time will propel you towards a greater freedom or it will enslave you back into past precipices. In this energy, you have the opportunity to reprogram the childhood emotions into a powerful force that will empower the emotional adult that you are becoming, and to recognize the emotional belief system that you carry within and decide what belongs to you and what doesn't belong there anymore. In so doing, you "Dragon Step Forward, Parry and Punch," determined to resolve old mistreatments and establish a new emotional Self.

35- Grasp the Sparrow's Tail / Responsibility

As you go through the disintegration of your old emotional patterns, a new realization is coming forth, the insight that you are more that what you created in your past. As you "Grasp the Sparrow's Tail" from this innovative perspective, you grasp at the nobility of your spirit with the willpower of committing to recognize who you are, and the truth of who you are. You are stepping into the energy of 35, and the self-reliance of the number 5 represents taking your responsibility for the recurrent patterns that you chose to settle into from the past, and be willing to face the excuses, the denial or the victim attitude that you might still use when you do not have the courage or valor to make those changes. So once again, you seek, within the graciousness of your spirit, the bravery of your heart and the truth that will set you free. You commit to rely upon the true self, the self closer to your Spiritual nature, willing to be responsible for making empowered choices. You face the past patterns and who you thought you were, and you reinvent yourself from a fresh place of love and acceptance, stepping closer to the vibration of your greater Self.

36- Single Whip / Self-Acceptance

When you have a new realization, you need to initiate it in all levels of your being. As you whip it through your bodies and into your reality, you bring it out into the world. "Single Whip" is a Yang movement that says to the world, "this is who I am, this is how I express myself from now on, and I want to honor, respect and value this new me. In a single intent, I whip it into my world and I allow the power of my spirit to manifest the truth of who I am becoming". You are now under the influence of the number 6 combined with the power of 3, and that Spiritual energy is carrying you, through your duality, to manifest your genuine self. You are now able to embrace the duality of your emotions without conflicts, accepting the vastness and variety of your emotions with a new awareness, with the power of self-love and self-acceptance. You "Single Whip" this realization of who you have become, your intent in alignment with your heart and actions.

37- Wave Hands like Clouds (9 times) / The Observer

As you step into the repetition of #37, you find yourself moving clouds. The clouds represent the thoughts coming through your mind, where you have an opportunity to ponder your new discoveries. Each time you "Wave Hands like Clouds," you step to the side, giving yourself a chance to look at your life from a contemplative place, moving the flow of your being in a linear way with your feet and in a circular fashion with your hands. Stepping aside to observe the current of your thoughts and emotions, you allow the repetition of "Wave Hands like Clouds" to focus on your journey from an inner awareness, where your thinking and your feelings align in the dance of your experiences. You are moving through the influence of the power of 3, the synergy of your mind and heart creating a space of inner reflection where the karmic influence of the #7 asks you to find that inner guidance that will light your way from the inside out, from a deep and true conviction of the heart to a wise and thoughtful expression in your life. You repeat this movement 9 times, for you are rebirthing yourself from within, moving through the old emotional karmic patterns into a freer sense of self.

38- Single Whip / Vision

It is with a clearer vision that you step into "Single Whip," for you are a changed person. You have delved into a depth of your being which has ignited a radiance from within, and you are ready to face the changes that arise from a whole new vantage point. In the energy of 38, the power of your convictions is carried through the momentum of change and infinite possibilities, where your vision has expanded to encompass more of your dreams and desires. You are now capable of foreseeing a greater you, feeling the hope of it in your heart and aligning this awareness with a sincerity of commitment. You have come to a resolution with your fears at that present time, and you are looking forward to the changes and new possibilities appearing on your horizon. As you "Single Whip" that joyful and powerful energy into your life, the journey continues to be the greatest discovery of your self.

39- High Pat the Horse / Freedom

As you 'High Pat the Horse," you meet with the power of the horse and its intrinsic desire for freedom. The horse is the power that freed humanity by helping all beings move and travel further, opening a whole new vision of space and changing the agricultural ways forever. From the freedom and power of the horse, human consciousness leaped forward and entered a new era. When you "High Pat the Horse," you are encouraging your power of freedom to come forth and change your perception. You are under the influence of 39, completing a cycle and rebirthing yourself with a renewed sense of power. You are freeing your self-imposed limitations, releasing the emotional dependency of old feelings to enter a freer space within your heart. You are stepping into a new sovereignty, a new sense of power within. As you "High Pat the Horse," you are aware as well as highly motivated to step into that new sense of freedom and experience the mightiness that it brings you. You are rebirthing yourself into the adult that you are becoming, healing and completing one of the many paths you chose to experience, sometimes coming from a very far away past. As you face these old patterns, you recognize that you have a choice, a choice of carrying burdening memories and suffering through the old, or a choice of forgiving yourself and all, and freeing your powers to manifest your dreams and visions.

40- Separate Right Foot / The Manifestor

As you align yourself with your chosen path, you find yourself into a whole new energy wave, for you are now under the influence of the number 4- the Manifestor, the energy of Earth, matter, materialization- and you are starting to manifest a variety of experiences that you need to go through in order to become that freer Self, in order to evidence that expanded Self. The zero of infinite energy, of pure consciousness multiplies this intention, and whatever you manifest now is bringing you closer to comprehend and follow your path of freedom. In "Separate Right Foot," you are kicking with a yearning to expand yourself. It is a movement of action. It is the direction of the will. You are separating your right foot in North East direction. You are spreading your intention and aligning it with your will and the Higher Will of your Soul. You are reaching out, standing on one foot, wanting to find a new center, a new equilibrium within yourself, a new challenge of standing in a different center within. Through this gravitational pull, you also find that your emotional center is shifting into a whole new awareness. The old emotional place where you felt comfortable, albeit unfulfilled, has disappeared, and you are now exploring the feelings of centering within emotionally, feeling your equilibrium secure from within.

41- Separate Left Foot / Standing in Duality

As you discover your new center, between Yin and Yang, left and right, between your ability to be intuitive as well as creative, you step into #41 to harmonize your center of power, your center line. As you "Separate Left Foot," you expand into the North-West direction, the direction of change. You expand into your intuition, the inner voice guiding you to remember your balance within this newfound freedom. Your emotional self wants to be nurtured, supported and loved, so you expand into your Yin energy, the feminine power within. In the number 40, it was important to be creative and reach the outside world. With 41, it is important to be receptive to your intentional wisdom. You are under the influence of the #1, the self, the individual mind, trying to find a new emotional center within. You acknowledge that in order to achieve this balance, you need to step into the Middle Way and to harmonize the Yin and Yang within yourself. As you "Separate Left Foot," you realize your ability to stand in your duality, accepting your emotional self and a new awareness of the limitless possibilities of your heart.

42- Turn Around & Kick (Left Foot)/ Expanding the New Self

In the search for your emotional center, there is a need to "Turn Around and Kick" forward. You are expanding yourself in all directions in order to find a new center, so in your turn around, you allow yourself to look back and kick in the direction of the South, the direction of joy and love. This is an expansion of Yang energy, you are kicking forward, willing to extend yourself with a joyful intention, in order to manifest this new awareness.

In the previous 40 and 41, you separated your right and left foot into the corner positions, searching for balance within the self. Now you are standing into the warrior energy, looking back and willing to expand even more into your new emotional self. You are under the influence of #2, the duality of your heart manifesting in a stronger way each time, in order to give you the opportunities to release the old, to step into the new and find your center within, from a loving and joyful place.

43- Brush Knee and Step Forward (L)/

44- Brush Knee and Step Forward (R)/
   Emotional Harmony

In the expansion of your newly found emotional center, you then "Brush Knee and Step Forward." You are willing to continue to walk that path and experience what is to come. You walk both ways, left and right, with the energies of 3 & 4 carrying you forward into that new recognition. The energy and power of 3 help you brush anything that will stand in your way, that will hold you back, and the power of manifestation of the number 4 concretize your intention and your desire for emotional harmony within. You go forward, balancing left and right, feeling this centering, grounding it within yourself, experiencing it physically, emotionally and mentally with determination and a renewed sense of hope. Each time you step into that awareness, each time you allow yourself to reconsider who you are and what you feel, you come closer to the greatness of your Spiritual Being.

45- Step Forward and Punch Downward / Courage

By continuing to go forward, you realize and accept that you can rely upon this new identity of your self. The energy of 5 gives you the ability to respond to the new awareness of who you are. This brings some changes, some new adjustments to be acquired. As you "Step Forward and Punch Downward," you are going forward with an intention of blocking and punching what you find on your path. You also punch downward toward the Earth, grounding your desire to manifest who you are in physical form, willing to withstand any necessary physical confrontations in order to birth that new self into your reality. With a renewed sense of self, you "Step Forward and Punch Downward", relying on the truth and the trust that you hold within, to walk your path from a new perspective and to be bold and courageous in facing the challenges you might encounter.

46- Turn Around and Whip Punch / Resolution

With the desire to manifest even more of who you are, the call of your Spirit is guiding you to "Turn Around and Whip Punch." In order to go forward, you are faced once again with the need to look at your shadow. Any unresolved emotional residue will be exposed at this time, for the energy of 4 is manifesting that which is in need of completion. Deep emotions are bubbling up to the surface, feelings buried through the busy times of your earlier life. Now, the energy of 6, your spiritual guidance, is wanting to clear the emotional self at a deep level so any loose ends have to be examined, reflected upon and healed. It is a time of facing your very own truth, aligning your actions with your desires and your Soul's purpose. You "Turn Around and Whip Punch" with force, determination and courage, for this is not a time of idleness or reverie. In this moment of heartfelt certainty, you are lead forward on your chosen path.

47- Dragon Step Forward, Parry and Punch / Karmic Retribution

In your intent to realign your actions with your innate truth, you now embody the energy of the Dragon, where you have the vision of all aspects of yourself, the facets of your mind and the consequences of your actions. The karmic influence of 7 is upon you once again, and this time, you are looking at your life and realizing all the feelings and emotions that have brought you to this place in time. With the Dragon's power, you recognize the emotional patterns you have been reacting to for a very long time. The #7 reminds you where and how you have fallen back into the familiar, creating a deep rut that is now accumulating into an emotional dead end. Unresolved issues are now becoming a weight that you find yourself wanting to lift off your shoulders, off your heart. The Dragon reminds you of all that you are, and all that you can become if you choose to let go of the repetitive unhealthy patterns that do not serve you anymore. It is a moment of self-realization, where the courage to follow your truth will empower your actions from now on. You "Dragon Step Forward, Parry and Punch" these very entrenched habitual patterns, understanding that you continuously initiate change through your karmic retribution when you make the choice of realigning your intention with your Soul's purpose.

48- Kick with Right Foot / Equilibrium

You are now in a position where you have to find a new balance. You have realized the need to move beyond old emotions, and you "Kick with Right Foot" in a new direction, trying to find your center again. The energy of #8 brings the movement of change, and the change of heart that you are experiencing is asking you to muster your courage to kick forward against doubts, uncertainties and fears. To create the equilibrium between the truth of your heart and the physical actions needed in your life, you challenge the familiar and you "Kick with

Right Foot," determined to discover an inner place of harmonic flow where you will be able to manifest the sincerity of your desires.

49- Taming the Tiger Stance / Taming the Fears

The archetypal energy of the Tiger brings your fears to the surface with the need to confront them. As you choose to face your fears, you are also able to tame your fears. With the energy of #9, you are rebirthing yourself into a new emotional being. You have come to understand the necessity to challenge and subdue what has been controlling you for a very long time. As long as you give power to your fears, you realize that you will never be free to be and manifest your highest potential. The energy of #4 calls you now to take charge of your fears, the fear of not being good enough, the fear of not being capable of creating your dreams, your fear of the unknown, your fear of lack and all the other fears attached to your past. It is a time of mastering the courage to alter all fears in order to rebirth yourself anew, to know what it would feel like to live without fear in a world you could trust.

50- Strike the Tiger to the Left/

51- Strike the Tiger to the Right/ Negative Ego

As you "Strike the Tiger Left and Right" the energy of 5- your self reliance- is called forth in order to continue to face your fears. When you "Strike the Tiger to the Left," you strike the emotional upheaval created by your fears, you take on the responsibility of fighting your negative ego which holds you in a state of fearfulness. It is as if all you knew about your inner self has come apart, the zero of fifty encompassing the universal truth of the circle, where you have to redefine who you believe yourself to be. When you then "Strike the Tiger to the Right," you disempower your negative ego holding your mind in a state of denial and fright. With the energy of the #1, the beliefs you hold about your self are now being challenged. Who you thought you were suddenly has shifted, and in the inner battle of your mind, you realize that being self-reliant means more than just taking care of the physical self. It means having a hold on your dreadful thoughts and being willing to strike the fears out in order to acquire a new self-esteem, a trust in your capacities that nothing or no one can ever make you doubt of.

52- Kick with Right Foot / Polarity

As you continue to advance through the dense and intense emotional turmoil of your being, you "Kick with Right Foot," continuously trying to create a new balance. You are now in the energy of 52, and the duality of your mind and heart bring forth the warrior in you. This duality makes you realize that it is not only your belief system in need to change, it is also the constant roller coaster you find yourself in emotionally. You are now fully aware that your dual nature creates a polarity within that needs to be anchored in the courage to confront deep-seated fears and the wisdom to grow with it. You "Kick with Right Foot", a Yang movement that reestablishes your self-reliance as you continue your commitment to establish your inner peace.

53- Double Wind Fills the Ears / Internal Dialogue

The power of your momentum brings you to "Double Wind Fills the Ears, striking with both fists. You have made a choice to reach as far and as high as you can in order to move the stagnant emotional Qi of your being. The energy of 3 is now focused as an arrow with a target that you want to reach with both fists. Your intention springs out to move the wind around you and in you, the wind representing the thoughts that are constantly running through your mind. Reaching the ears makes you listen to your internal dialogue, where you feel the depth of your emotions and the powerful impact of your thoughts. With a double intent, you extend yourself further and face your opponent, an opponent who exists in the recesses of your mind and heart. It is a time of action, where your willingness to face your struggle of identity will assist you in reaching a greater level of fusion of heart and mind along your journey of love.

54- Kick with Left Foot/

55- Turn Around and Kick with Right Foot/ Self-Reliance

As you continue to face your negative ego, it becomes imperative to be willing to kick left and right, to face this internal turmoil with all your might. You are now under the energies of 4 and 5, where your inner fears and struggles are manifesting themselves into your life, for they are now an energy that is coming forward, blocking the flow of your desires and your ability to create in accordance with your will. With the double energy of 55, your self-reliance becomes your self-realization. How close are you from manifesting your dreams? How sincere are you in standing in the truth of your being? These questions raise the desire to take action, to break through a long time of unresolved fears and uncertainties. You "Kick with Left Foot", willing to face the imbalances of your heart, then you "Turn Around and Kick with Right Foot" kicking the mental beliefs you thought were the foundations of your self, for you realize these have become a wall impeding your view on your path of freedom, on your path of self realization. You are now facing a new direction in your life.

56- Dragon Step Forward, Parry and Punch / Healing the Past

As you emerge through this self realization, all of your past experiences and certainties about who you were are shifting into a new level of awareness. With the energy of 56, your spiritual guidance is now also involved in creating your awakening. You are not only recognizing your deepest fears and beliefs that do not serve you anymore, you are also seeing your life from the perspective of the Dragon. You are the sum total of all the lives you have ever lived, and this realization brings a new vision and scope of the entrenched patterns you have been desiring to change for a very long time. You "Dragon Step Forward, Parry and Punch," knowing that you are not only fighting old patterns from this lifetime but a karmic effect that has been with you for a very long time. You understand that by transforming negative aspects of your self into a positive force in your present reality, you are also reaching to all your "past realities" and healing the wounds of long ago.

57- Withdraw and Push / Self-Awakened Mind

As you "Withdraw and Push", the karmic influence of your past has now reached a place where you find yourself wanting to withdraw before continuing forward. After facing the different aspects of your fears, you now need to absorb the shock and you withdraw to reach a centered place, once again, for the karmic energy has gained momentum and asks you to consider your new choices. Your ability to respond to this new wave of energy is going to demand your attention in order not to repeat or fall back into old and familiar ways. Under the energy of 7, the Law of Cause and Effect is showing you the struggle you just went through, and you realize that your next move will create the possible future of your life. In standing in the power of your self-awakened mind, you withdraw and contemplate your next move and you push against any residue of doubt or fear you still sense within yourself.

58- Cross Hands / Crossroad

You are now stepping into "Cross Hands," and the energy of #8 gives you all options to consider. The internal changes of your heart have brought you to stand with a new vision of yourself, emotionally and mentally. "Cross Hands" symbolizes standing at a crossroad of your life where you can create a new path if you accept the changes without fear, or you can choose to walk the familiar path of your past where you enter once again in the Karmic Wheel of unresolved emotions. The courage to take your emotional self in charge is what will make the difference between the lessons learned and the unfinished ones. As you "Cross Hands," you align with your deeper truth, a heartfelt truth, where you can choose to be the adult healing the child within. You have found yourself at this crossroad before, but the sensitivity and understanding of your emotional past bring you an opened and potential vision of your present choices. Limitless possibilities are opening their doors, for the #8 holds the energy of the infinite, and with it comes the dawn of a new day, a reaching deep into the Self to feel and claim that which is yours, the possibility of loving forgiveness, peace within, and the acknowledgment of the heartfelt dream of the Soul.

SECTION 3/UNITY

Section 3 unfolds into bringing the alignment of your Mind, Heart and Body through the embodiment of the Higher Frequencies of your Soul, Unconditional Love and Sacred Vessel. With section 3, you are under the power of the Trinity, the Divine Unity expressed into matter through the duality of Yin and Yang. The energy and power combined give your journey a stronger determination with a new course. You have walked through the terrain of your life, growing through the physical body and its needs for balance, feeling the emotional body with its desires and fears, and discovering the mental body and its willpower. Section 3 offers the reawakening of your Spiritual body, where your understanding and realization are guided from your Soul and Spirit. It is this greater force in you that is showing you the way. Your body is manifesting the results of your beliefs, your heart is given the opportunity to make decisions with loving intent, and your mind yearns for the fulfillment of your Soul's journey. Here at this crossroad, the Light of the Higher Self illuminates the dreams of the physical Self and the choices you make will direct you towards these dreams or will make you step once again into the Karmic Wheel of past experiences still needing to be transcended. "Do you think, feel and act upon this physical plane with integrity, reverence and gratitude for your life and all life?"

These considerations will be explored in Section 3.

Section 3 includes 29 moves. 2+9=11=Master number of Revelation of the fusion of physical self with Spiritual Self, where the duality of 2 is embraced and integrated into the Oneness/Wholeness of your experience.

59- Embrace Tiger and Return to the Mountain / Emergence

You are now at the dawn of a spiritual emergence. Under the energy of #9, you are completing a cycle and rebirthing yourself into a new light. The cycle of soul and substance that have delineated your journey until now is being raised to the cycle of Spirit and Light, and with it you face the Tiger once again, and the fears rising from this new place. "You Embrace the Tiger," for you now realize that your fears of Self, of life, are stepping stones helping you climb the mountain of your dreams. You "Embrace Tiger and Return to the Mountain" of your life, seeing with a new vision, taking charge of the emotional baggage you are bringing with you. Seeing and sensing with your spiritual awareness opens a whole new understanding of your karmic lessons. The fears that bind you in a certain state of mind and action are now perceived in their truer light and their power is beginning to crumble. Completing this cycle means unlocking the ability to respond to those fears and lifting yourself in a new resolution of heart and mind.

60- Grasp the Sparrow's Tail Diagonal / Gate of Understanding

With the energy of 60, your Spiritual Self becomes ever more empowered within your awareness. You "Grasp the Sparrow's Tail Diagonal" and with it you turn to view your path in a different direction. The strength and endurance needed for the journey are sustained by the lifting of your Spirit. Somehow your life has a new meaning, and you call forth the nobility of your Spirit to guide you further. You "Grasp the Sparrow's Tail Diagonal" with renewed hope, with the #0 of universal forces magnifying your choices.

You are going through a Spiritual Emergence, where everything has changed in your consciousness and your will to live combined with your desire to find the truth within have opened the gates of Spiritual Understanding. You repeat a familiar pattern, "Grasp the Sparrow's Tail Diagonal", to comprehend the changes within so that, from now on, your Higher Self will be heard, felt and honored on your path of Self Realization.

61- Diagonal Single Whip / Creating the Dream

With the determination, you step into the energy of "Diagonal Single Whip." This is a powerful move, Yang in nature, where you want to affirm your choices in a new direction, in a committed way and empowered frequency. You are now under the influence of the #1, the self growing into the consciousness of the Higher Self, feeling the puissance of standing in your truth to carry forth that which is essential to your more authentic Self. You have felt for a very long time the limitations of being human trying to manifest your Soul's purpose, but as you receive the influence of 6 and1 combined, you are now allowing your inner Self the possibility of reaching out to the world and creating a piece of the dream at one with you. It is with a revived resoluteness, bravery and perception that you now whip and act out these energies into your life.

62- Wild Horse Parts its Mane (R)/

63- Wild Horse Parts its Mane (L)/

64- Wild Horse Parts its Mane (R)/ Journey of the Soul

It is with a new sense of freedom that you now step into "Wild Horse Parts its Mane." It is exhilarating to find yourself on a new course, being wild and free to feel the changes occurring in your life. You are now going forward, and the wild horse is galloping towards a new venture, where the duality of your mind has centered into one destination, where the power and energy of your conviction help you brush aside any doubts, and where the desire to take action is fueled by the vision of freedom. With "Wild Horse Parts its Mane", you free yourself, for a moment in time, of your fears and of old constraining thoughts. You realize that there is something else waiting for you on your journey and you are willing to take the steps right, left, right to experience this guidance and inner knowing from within, exhilarated and joyful, with nothing to stop you. Like the horse that instinctively runs for its freedom, you advance with a stronger capacity, willing to part from any past assumption you ever carried, to allow the meaningful and beautiful journey of your Soul to rise as a new dawn.

65- Grasp the Sparrow's Tail / Uniqueness

It is with an eager understanding that you step into "Grasp the Sparrow's Tail", and under the energy of #5, you are now wanting to clasp the tail of your life and follow it back to its original intent, where you are embracing your virtues, your talents, your gifts and lifting your visions and hopes into the Light. You are receiving the spiritual input of your Higher Self and you choose to take hold of the opportunities coming your way. Your trust and self-reliance are growing within and you are capable of honoring the uniqueness of your being. As you "Grasp the Sparrow's Tail," the noble cause of your Spirit resonates throughout your physical journey.

66- Single Whip / Following the Golden Path

With the energy of double 6, the guidance of your spiritual awareness leads you to assert your newfound freedom. As you stand in "Single Whip," you look like the archer ready to shoot the arrow, with powerful intent and clear direction. The Yang energy of your whip confirms your commitment to follow the call of your Soul, to whip forth, with diligence and valor, upon the path of highest fulfillment. It is a time of great insight, where your inner voice is clear and strong, where the doubts of your mind have quiet down and the effortlessness of your decisions allow you to "Single Whip" with precision and clarity onto the Golden Path of the great adventure of your life.

67- Fair Lady Weaves the Shuttle (SE)

68- Fair Lady Weaves the Shuttle (NE)

69- Fair Lady Weaves the Shuttle (NW)

70- Fair Lady Weaves the Shuttle (SW)
Weaving the Golden Thread

As your journey unfolds, you weave the golden thread of realization through the tapestry of your experiences. It is a time of building new foundations based on spiritual recognition, so "Fair Lady Weaves the Shuttle" in the 4 complementary directions.

With the energy of 7, you turn to the South East where the Dragon's energy contemplates. Under the influence of karmic retribution, you are becoming more of who you are, for Dragon allows you to envision your human self as the sum total of all your experiences, and within that vision, a new thread of integration appears upon the canvas of your artistry. With the energy of 8, you turn to the North East where the spirit of Sparrow shines. It is with your will that you will continue to weave the knowledge of your realization upon your life, and it is with your willingness to change and grow that you will be able to create and harvest the fruits of your labor. With the energy of 9, you turn to the North West, where Monkey's presence reminds you to be flexible and on the move. You are coming to the end of a cycle of emotional breakthrough and you are being rebirthed into a new cycle of spiritual realization. Your mind needs to be alert and your Soul calls for flexibility in the belief system so that you may weave the shuttle with a renewed intention. With the energy of 7 and 0, you turn to the South West where the Cock stands proudly. It is with valor and courage that you continue to face the karmic resonance of your choices. The Cock reminds you to stand in your truth honorably, for to change your karmic destiny, you will need to weave valor into your convictions, sincerity into your commitments and fearlessness in shining the true colors and brightness of your personal and unique gifts to the World. You weave the shuttle, aware that every thread reflects the gold of your integrity and the wisdom of your spiritual ancestry.

71- Grasp the Sparrow's Tail / Harvest

You are now under the influence of the retribution of the Law of Cause and Effect. By standing in the individual power that you are becoming, you once again ward-off the karmic past and face the challenges to come. You roll back to grasp a new perspective of the possibilities your life is offering you. You press against the sluggish energy of old familiar patterns and you push forward, ready to face the consequences of actions accumulated until now. The human self is feeling taller and stronger with your ability to respond for all those past actions, and you are growing steadily into your greater Self. At this point, there are no more excuses for delaying the changes necessary to come closer to the happiness and peace you have been searching for so long. So you "Grasp the Sparrow's Tail" with the realization of your inner self wanting to match the guidance of your Higher Self. You are now reaping the harvest of your past thoughts, feelings and deeds in order to reach this higher vibration within.

72- Single Whip / Soul Magic

You are now influenced by the duality of karmic energy. Your newfound understanding is confronted with the old belief system. How much of your desire to change are you going to be able to whip into your life? How much of your convictions and insights will you be able to refine into your future? How clear is the vision of your new Self and how strong is the pull of the old one? All of these influences are present as you "Single Whip." It is a vulnerable time, even though this is a Yang movement. It is susceptible because in the search of balance within duality, there is often a tendency to sway to the extremes before finding one's center. The old and familiar weighs on one side of the scale, and the new possibilities are just starting to appear and create a different reality. Nonetheless, you step into "Single Whip," aiming to manifest the magic of your Soul into the mystery of your destiny.

73- Wave Hands Like Clouds (7 times) / Tear the Veil

As you step into the flow of "Wave Hands Like Clouds," the time has come to reflect deeply on the direction you are giving your life. Like clouds, your thoughts wave many images through your inner gaze. As you step side to side, the Karmic Law of Cause and Effect unveils in front of your eyes. The power of your thinking process is accentuated by the energies repeated 7 times. It is as if a veil is being torn and an opening of clear consciousness is allowing the light of understanding to clarify your direction and your purpose. What you thought was forgotten or resolved is now coming into full focus, for the Karmic Law doesn't allow for unfinished or incomplete experiences. Through the labyrinth of your mind, you search to remember and ponder the deeper significance of the causes made in the past and the learning of the effects in your present reality.

74- Single Whip / Mental Strength

Your desire to manifest your new understanding and conviction is getting stronger. You are committed to bring forth the hidden thoughts and feelings that might hinder your progress. You "Single Whip" with the intention to bring everything to the surface, to be able to work with this karmic past and transform it when necessary. The spiritual force guiding you is joined with the Earth power of the energy of 4 supporting you. It is a time to balance the creative self and to carry that leadership into your life. The emotional release now experienced is supported by the mental resolution of choosing new ways of feeling and acting. You "Single Whip" one more time, making new decisions, new choices which bring you closer to the truth of your visions, to the integrity of your Spirit.

75- Snake Creeps Down / Letting Go

You are now entering into the deep transformation of snake energy. In order to grow into who you are, you find yourself needing to let go of the old and familiar boundaries you placed yourself into for a very long time. As the "Snake Creeps Down," it reaches a profound emotional place where the poison of past addictive behaviors, of complacent thinking and weakened will are being dislodged and brought to the Light. In your desire to become self-reliant in all aspects of your being, there is a need to outgrow the old behavioral patterns, the old cloak you wore in front of the world and the illusion you carried within. It is a time of death and rebirth, of changing poison into medicine, of facing deep-seated beliefs and emotional cope out that you can't deny anymore. As the "Snake Creeps Down," it brings up from the depth of your Soul the opportunity to shed your old skin and to rebirth yourself into a much truer self, a self willing to take responsibility for all aspects of your life, dark and light balancing themselves in an embrace of love and renewal.

76- Golden Cock Stands on One Leg (L)/

77- Golden Cock Stands on One Leg (R)/ New Dawn

As you emerge from the transformation of the snake, the pride of your colors shines in the brightness of a new dawn. You are now standing in the energy of the "Golden Cock Stands on One Leg", which calls on resurrecting the new Self, proudly showing your new equilibrium and a new state of balance. The golden shine of your emergence reflects a watchfulness and presence guided by Divine Intelligence. Under the energy of 6, your Spiritual Light helps you perceive the need to find a new center. Standing on one leg is searching for the renewal of hope in a proud display of physical skills. Under the energy of 7, as you face your karmic experiences, you find the strength and courage to stand facing your destiny. The energies of double 7 are powerful, calling on you to rebirth yourself from the old into a proud, fertile and colorful manifestation. As the "Golden Cock Stands on One Leg ", the resurrection of your Soul heralds the dawn of illumination.

78- Step Back and Repulse Monkey (L)

79- Step Back and Repulse Monkey (R)

80- Step Back and Repulse Monkey (L) Illusion

It is important to take the time to reflect when you are facing such great changes. As you "Step Back and Repulse Monkey", you allow the mind to encompass all that has happened. With the energy of 8, your mind needs to stretch to fathom the changes of your being and to embrace these changes without fear. With the energy of 9, you are completing a deep karmic cycle and your understanding is combined with your willingness to expand upon the unresolved. Then you step into the energies of 8 and 0, entering a phase of your life where all your foundations and your belief systems are forced to change, to grow, to turn upside down and to twist in different directions. The challenge now is to trust that the new Self emerging from this chaos is your greater Self guiding you to a place of spiritual vision, emotional freedom and physical accomplishments. You have to face the instability of the mind, the trickeries of illusion, the influence of the negative ego, so you "Step Back and Repulse Monkey," giving yourself the opportunity to contemplate where your mental processes are leading you.

81- Diagonal Flying / Valor

Under the influence of 81, you "Diagonal Flying", the self seeks to deploy its wings in a wider fashion, desiring to experience its new freedom of thought and emotion and how it feels changed because of it. You stand in the South- West where the powers of the Cock bring valor and courage to your flight. You are starting a new journey within, and "Diagonal Flying" gives you a different view, a higher perspective of your destination. Your reach has become extensive, your dreams are finally looming over the horizon, and your self-confidence allows your visions to soar. Within the profound inner changes of your being, you are finding a core place where you can stretch into the limitless possibilities your greater purpose is guiding you to. You fly with determination and valor as your wings unfold with new meaning and hope.

82- Lift Hands and Step Up / Self-Expression

In the journey of self-discovery, the powers of Heaven and Earth are always embracing you. As you "Lift Hands and Step Up", you reach to the Spirit and Cosmic Source to enlighten you on this path. You allow the flow of Heavenly guidance to confirm the visions of your Higher Self, for the dreams you cherish need to align themselves with your Cosmic Destiny. As you step up, the Earth powers beneath you support and nurture your desires and hopes to manifest those dreams. The nature of duality of your being is now aligning itself with the polarization of Spirit and Soul, integrating the greater Yang and the Greater Yin. These dimensions of Light and substance are manifesting through your intentions, your commitments and the agreement to recreate upon the physical plane the unlimited expression of your Spiritual Essence. You "Lift Hands and Step Up" joining these complementary opposites into a joyous dance of self-expression.

83- White Crane Spreads its Wings / Sacred Reverence

With the influence of infinite possibilities coming from #8, you stand in the white crane energy once again. The immortality of your Soul becomes more apparent each time you stand in alignment with Spirit. As you step into the white crane, the purity of your intention reveals the consecrated place you find yourself in. Spreading your wings, you deploy your inner truth and virtues to the world. With the power of 3, you can fly approaching your spiritual commitment that is guiding you from above and within. From that vantage place, you can see your life extending further into the future where your dreams and visions are emerging into your reality. You understand that, in the infinity of your existence, if you follow the truth of your heart, honor the teachings of your past experiences and remember the grace of your journey, you will be able to manifest the dream that you not only desire but is the greatest growth for your Soul. You "White Crane

Spreads its Wings" with pure intent and sacred reverence on a limitless and hopeful horizon.

84- Brush Knee and Step Forward (L) / Self-Doubt

As you "Brush Knee and Step Forward," you are bringing these energies down to Earth, and you now step forward wanting to brush whatever opposition comes your way. You recognize that your greatest adversary is your own negative ego, that voice within whispering that you are not good enough, or you can't have it all, you don't deserve, you can't possibly manifest your aspirations. This is the challenge you now face, your own fears and feelings of inadequacy, so you brush them aside, and you forge ahead, knowing that you can't stop half way, that if you don't listen to the call of your Soul, a part of you will die, and your creative self will shrink and become dormant again. With the longing to manifest your expectations, you step forward on the journey of creation, in the adventure of choosing each step, each breath and each realization leading you on your visionary path.

85- Needle at Sea Bottom / Self-Love

In the whirlwind of changes you find yourself into, you are looking for the compass of your heart, the needle that you know you must follow in order to be true to your Soul's yearning. You delve into the depths of your emotions, searching for something to grab onto, a center place among the waves of your hopes and desires, a calmer shore on the sea of your life. This is a time to trust your inner knowing, for the ability to reach within and without is there with the power of 5. There is a peaceful center within the turbulence of the emotions, and you now want to reach deep within to find that very thin needle which intends to guide you deeper within the flux of your feelings. You "Needle at Sea Bottom" finding the patience to observe the troubled waters of your experiences and the murkiness of an agitated heart. With great compassion, you allow the jetsam and flotsam of your emotional consciousness to settle into a clearer flow, where you can now find the needle of a self-reliant heart pointing in the direction of a truthful current of self-love.

86- Fan Through Back / Self-Empowerment

With a heartfelt commitment, you emerge from the depths of your emotions into "Fan Through Back." Under the influence of 6, your spiritual journey becomes clearer and the certainty of your mind fans itself with power, stepping forward to display this new realization. It is a time to stand in your life with conviction and commitment, a time where the power of your backbone needs to uphold your beliefs and decisions. The flow of your unending thoughts is expressed in the fan you present yourself with. You stand courageously in a place where you allow yourself to be seen, to be vulnerable, to be heard. You have grown from an uncertain to a more secure and trustworthy state of mind. Among the constant changes lived through the energy of 8, you are learning to trust your inner voice, the guidance of your Soul, so you may display with confidence the kaleidoscope of your belief system which you are able to fan with power and an upright integrity.

87- White Snake Turns Body and Strikes / White Medicine

As you step into the energy of the white snake, the past transformation of karmic issues has been turned into a white medicine. As the "White Snake Turns Body and Strikes," the poison of the negative ego and the fears attached to it are being discharged out of you. You are under the influence of 7, the manifestation of Cause and Effect, and your renewed dedication to Spirit allows you to strike out the internal poison you carried within for so long. You have transmuted past karma into a force of clear white energy, and the snake's strike helps you shed your old skin and emerge into a joyful and pure light. You are now able to look back at your life and discard the familiar patterns of self-destructive thoughts. You not only discard those, you step into a whole new path, where heavy footprints are being erased with the awareness of your Soul's purpose and the willingness to become all you can ever be.

88- Dragon Step, Forward, Parry and Punch / Reincarnation

As you embody more of your Higher Self, the infinite changes of your life are bringing back memories of all your lifetimes. With the energy of the Dragon, you have moments of "déjà vu" where it seems you can transport yourself through time and space, where dimensions merge into one another, where the experiences of yesterday have become the feelings of today and the growth of tomorrow. You are in the energy of 8 Square and the forces of this current are bringing you remembrances of the continuity of your choices and the greatness of the part you play in the Universe. You are starting to grasp the impact of your physical journey in terms of the influence of your Soul upon all sentient living things and beings, the awesome responsibility of being a creator and created simultaneously with Divine Essence, and the unconditional acceptance of All That Is. You are able to lift yourself out of the personal ego into the Universal Oneness and as you "Dragon Step, Forward, Parry and Punch," the limitless consciousness of your Spirit is able to rejoice into this great flow of life and death, of Yang and Yin, of light and dark. The spirals of the energies of 8 are revealing to you all facets of your lives, past, present, future, and with the Dragon's power, you access all the potentials, talents and virtues you already possess. This is the knowledge of the Dragon, and you are ultimately able to embrace it and revere the sacredness of your eternal existence.

89- Step Forward, Grasp the Sparrow's Tail / Gift of Life

You now step into "Grasp the Sparrow's Tail" and the understanding of your spiritual path is helping you complete a part of the journey.

You are undergoing a rebirthing process, where you need to grasp the clear and pure nobleness of your Spirit, for you cannot go back to old emotional fears and uncertainties. You have become aware that, as you claim your part in the cosmic play, you own your choices and honor your Soul's commitment to bring forth the light you carry with the indestructible joy you feel welling from within. In the changing unknown, you grasp what is becoming real for you, the perceptive vision you are foreseeing, the love of your aspirations to co-create with the universal forces and the caring kindness of a beautiful world in which to share your light. It is a powerful time of recognition and appreciation for the gift of life you have received, and you now want to give a gift of Self. You "Grasp the Sparrow's Tail" calling on the sacredness of your Essence and the unconditional love of your heart to rebirth yourself into the gift of your presence.

90- Single Whip / Co-Creation

It is with the whip of intention that you step into the energy of 9 and 0. You have completed a cycle of transformation and you are now rebirthing yourself as the spiritual adult you always wanted to be. The universal force of zero is also the womb of your potentials and virtues. It nurtures and encompasses every aspect of your Spirit so you can master the Being of Light you already are. Within the circle of creation, you have mapped your life path through many rebirthings and now the urge to co-create with your spiritual awareness is greater than ever. Supported by the universal powers and all of its guidance, your focus on bringing the new Self into expression is unwavering. The flow of your consciousness is able to match the greater plan of your Soul and in this "Single Whip" you assert to the world and to yourself that you are ready to undertake a new journey where the emotional self is willing to embrace self-love, and where the mental self is able to fulfill a facet of self-realization.

91- Wave Hands Like Clouds (5 times) / Hermit's Journey

With each commitment made in the mind comes the need to internalize each one of these into the heart. As you "Wave Hands Like Clouds," you are starting an inner exploration where the comprehension of your experiences needs to be embodied as a truth resonating in the heart field. It is not enough to have an "aha experience" where you finally comprehend a greater part of your Self. This understanding has to be felt as an inner knowing in the greater depth of your being so that, in the silence of your inner sanctuary, you can find the voice of your unique perspective and claim it as your truth. This is the journey of the Hermit, where after acquiring many life experiences in the outer world, the Hermit visits the sacred temple of the inner world, and at one with Heart and Soul, he/she can extract the Light that will guide him/her toward its destiny. The power of 5 calls you to trust your thoughts and feelings, for your self-reliance and self-trust will enable you to proceed on the path of physical and emotional fulfillment illuminated by your spiritual essence.

92- Single Whip / Commitment

As you continue the rebirthing process, you find that your inner world of thoughts and feelings and your outer world of actions reflect a duality of expression. Your external manifestations do not yet correspond to your inner realization, so you need to whip and assess this energy into physical action. The experiences of the heart inspire you to bring forth a positive, clearer and stronger resolve to the new ways you aspire to establish in your outer world. With "Single Whip" you center these desires and hopes into the duality of your path. You now grasp the intensity of your choices and recognize that opposite forces are always at hand, and in the acknowledgement of both, you can find a center of focus, and you can trust yourself to navigate these emotional waters with a clarity of understanding and a body of determination.

93- High Pat the Horse / Angelic Presence

You are now feeling a higher level of freedom of expression as you step into "High Pat the Horse." With the power of 3, you are able to integrate a new vision with a calmer heart and to create a freer sense of Self. Your Spirit is helping you release the bondages of past karmic pains and your feelings of limitless possibilities open a euphoric state of consciousness. You are higher on the mountain of your life and you can envision a vast and colorful horizon, you can hear your Soul's voice singing, resonating in the truth of your heart, you can taste the winds of liberation from the pull of attachments and you can feel your oneness within the Cosmic rhythm. The Horse and its incredible power are allowing you to reach further, deeper within the aspirations of your Soul with a joy unknown or unfelt to you until now. As you strive to elevate your consciousness and illuminate your world with it, you have a glimpse of a blissful state of being, feeling like the touch of an angelic presence. For a moment in time, you are reborn from your ashes into the pure Light of your evolving Essence.

94- Cross Palms / Crossing Over

As you step into "Cross Palms," you reach out to bring forth this awareness into a more tangible energy. You are crossing over, from the Spiritual to the physical, from a sense of freedom to a desire for action. As you "Cross Palms," you direct your intention further up toward your dream, and further down toward its realization. You strive to complete a part of your journey where the first step of your newfound freedom needs to make an imprint upon the path of your life. With the energy of 4, the square, there is an integration of the circle of your life into the destination of your journey. Karmic past and present deeds are aligning to heal and co-create the You that you are becoming. You are making more conscious choices that leave a trail of causes behind you and open a hopeful space of possibilities in front of you. "Cross Palms" is crossing the wide river of your life, allowing yourself to swim with the currents of changes, recognizing the swirls of challenges to be faced, the jetsam and flotsam of stagnant pools of fears and doubts to be released, and feeling the support of the spirits of the waters- Undines- carrying you ever closer to the peaceful lake of an awakened heart.

95- Turn Around and Kick with Right Foot / Independence

As you step into the energy of 95, whatever is not completed will call your attention. As you grow into a clearer perception of your destiny, any loose ties to the past will need to be answered. You "Turn Around and Kick with Right Foot," kicking forward to continue to clear the way of your realization with determination and assertiveness. Any time you kick, you find yourself on one foot, challenging your center and commitment to honor the abilities and qualities of your Soul. Once again, in times of precarious balance, you need to trust in your capacity and capability to look deep within into the thoughts and feelings of inadequacy ingrained into your psyche, and courageously step up into your self-reliance and independence. As you turn around and face the negative ego that has been the foundation of your belief system, you kick it and allow it to crumble, so you may gather the facets of your Self where the greatness of your Spirit and the valor of your heart will harmonize with the sacred purpose of your Soul.

96- Step Forward and Punch Low / Pathways

You are now stepping into the energy of 6, the double triangle forming the six-pointed star. The energy of Spirit wants to descend into the expression of matter, where you can continue to evolve through the great rebirthing process you started. The Yang energy flows outward through action. The Yin energy centers inward through intuition. You are being guided to create new pathways where your self-empowerment will find expression in your life, and where your self-love will open new doors of possibilities within your reach. You "Step Forward and Punch Low," directing this energy towards the Earth, wanting to ground and root your choices into matter. There is an inner force that pushes you forward where doubts and uncertainties are confronted and where your inner wisdom illuminates your journey toward wholeness.

97- Step Forward and Grasp Sparrow's Tail / Source

Within the cyclic rhythm of Universal flow, you come into the energy of karma each time you hit #7, so past, present and future become one, in order to complete, heal and grow from all your experiences. As you step into "Grasp the Sparrow's Tail," you have been rebirthing yourself for quite a while and any unresolved issues will appear in a new perspective. You are now in a more objective space in looking at your past, for your Soul has been guiding you to recognize the patterns of physical actions and emotional dependency you leaned upon for so long. You are becoming fully aware of the nobility of your life, the graciousness of your existence unfolding itself as you continue your journey. The law of Cause and Effect resonates in your consciousness, and your willingness to forgive, accept, love and change brings anticipation in the aliveness of new possibilities. You understand that karma is not a punishment but the extraordinary flow of life and death through which you forever evolve, transform and awaken. As you are "Grasping at the Sparrow's Tail," you grab the link taking you back to your original Source of greatness, pure joy and Oneness.

98- Single Whip / Aiming to the Light

With the energy of 8, you are reminded that change is a constant flow that helps you move through your duality with infinite possibilities. Within this flow, you desire to find a new equilibrium, where you can aim and focus your awareness. You "Single Whip" standing in a posture where you aim to reach a target that will bring you closer to your inner core, your truth and the significance of your existence. It is the last "Single Whip" of your journey, where the intention of your will is combined with the desire to expand your visions into an infinite future. The target is a place of light, of peace and wisdom that appears to shine brighter each time you are willing to stretch the possibilities of your mind and embrace the changes of your heart.

99- Snake Creeps Down / Death of Initiation

As you step into 99, the energy of rebirthing is squared. Before you can rebirth yourself, you have to die to the old self. The snake is taking you on a final journey to shed any old skin, old garment, to complete the unfinished and to release the attachments and cords of karmic influence. It is the death of initiation, the Yin of letting go, the transmutation of the shadow. It is a death of all your belief systems, everything you believed to be true, the foundation upon which you built your perception of life. It is the death of your emotional excuses, weaknesses and self-pity. It is the death of the negative ego still trying to hold you back. It is the separation from the collective unconscious of fear and ignorance to a unique individual consciousness of love and wisdom. As you creep down through this process, the Snake teaches you how to transform toxicity into clarity, and how to surrender to the greater purpose of your existence. You are being challenged to your very core and your faith in yourself as well as in the universe is thoroughly tested. As you "Snake Creeps Down," you leave your old identity behind and you know you will never be the same as you surrender to the great truth of rebirthing yourself ever closer to the Divine Spirit that you are.

100- Step Up to Form 7 Stars / Heavenly Bodies

As you step into the energy of 100, your self is catapulted into the Heavenly Skies, and the individuality of your being is multiplied into infinite reflections. You are One with the universal forces that are transporting you into a journey of Holographic Expression. The power of 0 squared encompasses not only you and your earthly consciousness but also your Stellar origin with its infinite experiences into other worlds and other dimensions. You are joining the 7stars, the 7sisters of the Big Dipper, the constellation known for helping find the North direction. As the traveler on a sacred path, you step up to the new vision of yourself, calling on the powers of the stars to help direct your journey. You are now being guided to stand in All that you are, the One standing proudly next to the infinite consciousness of All That Is. You are, for a moment in time, able to grasp a glimpse of your multidimensionality, where the Light of your Higher Self shines brightly to show you North, to show you the way Home. You "Step Up to Form 7 Stars," encompassing all your karmic experiences into a new light of awakened realization and gratitude, where you understand that following the stars means following the journey of infinite creation that you are a sacred expression of.

101- Step Back to Ride Tiger / Higher Self

The earthly self is trying to match the energy of the Spiritual Self, separated by the 0 of universal awareness. The challenges you find within this intention refer to your fear of the unknown and your inability to trust your Higher Self. However, it is now time to "Step Back to Ride the Tiger" to get a handle on your fear, to step back and mount the roller coaster of emotions still surfacing in your heart. With the inner sight of your Spiritual self, you are capable of facing the shadow that has followed you all your life. You are now willing to shine the light in the deepest recesses of your heart and mind to confront and transform the forces of the dark that have held you back. You realize that dark energy was created through the perception of your belief systems and your emotional experiences. Your Higher Self is now giving you the confidence to ride and take a hold of this deep fear so you may step into your next adventure, where magic and physical reality will join to create a fearless and majestic expression of your being.

102- Turn Around and Sweep the Lotus / Spiritual Destiny

As you turn around, you find yourself in the duality of your being, represented by the Lotus frequency. The Lotus flower symbolizes the Law of Cause and Effect and represents the highest state of enlightened consciousness. Just like the Lotus blooms from a dark muddy swamp into a pure white flower, the duality of your consciousness falls and rises from forgetfulness to realization, from negativity to pure potentiality, from fear to love. In the awakening of your spiritual destiny, you accept that there cannot be a compromise between your thoughts and beliefs versus your actions and emotions. It is time to sweep the last remnants of beliefs holding you back to an old image of self, so that your Soul-Spirit connection may unfold and bloom into the fullness of your greater Self and you can manifest your essence in peaceful beauty and loving harmony. You "Turn Around and Sweep the Lotus," creating a wave within all aspects of your being, releasing your comfort zone to finally explore the infinite possibilities of aligning the One of Spirit standing with the Divine intent to manifest the One in Matter.

103- Shoot Tiger with Bow / Holographic Expression

As you emerge into a clear intention, you "Shoot Tiger with Bow." Your fears have finally surfaced into the light, so you may release them once and for all. The bow represents the Warrior/Knight within who intends to face and challenge these final doubts with courage and determination. As you "Shoot the Tiger" you release the arrow of self-realization into the shadow of your experiences. Your fears are shattered into pieces and the wholeness of the hologram of your truer self starts to appear in every facet, giving you a glimpse of the greatness of your being and the infinite power of your awakening. It is only with the willingness to die to the old image of self that you can reach an understanding of the magnificent Light you shine upon this plane. As you align the 1 mind, the 0 of essential creative source of your heart, and the power of action of the 3, you are able to take down the identity of who you thought you were and recreate the masterpiece of the artistry of your being, re-awakening to the mastery of your Soul's journey.

104- Dragon Step Forward, Parry and Punch / Spiritual Ancestry

As you "Dragon Step Forward, Parry and Punch," the multidimensionality of the Dragon appears in your consciousness. You are now pulling in all of the lifetimes of learning, healing, realization and growth you ever created. You are the sum total of all your experiences, and as you call forth the power of the Dragon, you access the Spiritual Ancestry of your past lives. All the talents, virtues and qualities you developed in the past are now at your reach and it is with this awareness that you "Step Forward, Parry and Punch." You are freeing yourself from the limited vision of your potential and capabilities and you are embracing the limitless possibilities of your dreams and purpose. Suddenly, you know it is all possible, for you walked trough your fears and challenged every one of them and you now step onto the other side, where self-love and self-realization open the threshold into a whole new dimension of your creative self. With the energy of 4, you manifest your powers of Spirit into matter, of a Being of Light recreating itself anew where the guidance of your Higher Self can finally fuse with the conscious awareness of your physical self.

105- Withdraw and Push / Path of Mastery

As the powerful energies of the Dragon transmute the memory of who you thought you were, you withdraw to internalize this process. This realization of your greater Self needs to be assimilated, understood and taken responsibility for. With the energy of 5, your self-reliance takes on a greater meaning, for you are now aware of your co-creation with the universal forces, and your ability to respond calls for a new commitment of your dreams and happiness. As you withdraw, you gather your power and your self-confidence and you push forward into the new vision of your life purpose. You are becoming the Master on your path of mastery, where you, the creator, chooses to embrace the responsibility of your life creation. As you "Withdraw and Push," you are entering into your self-empowerment where all experiences of the past are contributing to the foundation of the future you now know you create. Here you take on the journey of your life with excitement and the eagerness to start anew from a greater perspective, an inspired vision and an impeccable intent.

106-Cross Hands / Enlightenment

As you stand in "Cross Hands" posture, you are facing the East, once again, where the seed you nurtured at the beginning of this journey is now blooming into the Lotus of your enlightenment. Your Spirit, with the influence of 6, aligns itself with the Consciousness of the 1, the unique individual that you are, and your ability to embrace the limitless potential of your being, the 0, is fully activated. You now stand in the illumination of your Higher Self, and the road taken as well as the roads not taken unfold into a greater vision of your existence. You are bringing Spirit into matter, where the ideals of your Spiritual Self are able to project and create the golden path of the eternal adventure of your lives, reuniting your Spirit in the body physical, and illuminating your physicality in the perfection of Spirit. You "Cross Hands" in a prayer of joining Heaven and Earth to evoke the awakened human that you are, where the Light of unconditional love and compassionate acceptance traces the destiny and the evolution of your human experience with All.

107- Close Tai Chi / Heaven and Earth

The Karmic Wheel has turned a full circle, and under the energy of 7, you are now vibrating at a much higher frequency of awareness and compassion. The karma of Cause and Effect has brought you to the realization of your journey, where the physical experiences of your body, the emotional openings of your heart and the mental insights of your self-realization are all vibrating an octave higher within the limitless light, joy and grace of your Spirit. As you "Close Tai Chi", you stand, fully empowered with the consequences of your destiny, embracing the infinite and Cosmic Laws of growth and change and acknowledging your playful part in it. You free yourself from the helplessness of ignorance and rebirth yourself into the forever joyful consciousness of the gift of Life in all its manifestations. You understand that Tai Chi, the Supreme Polarity of your being, fueled by cosmic love, closes one chapter of the book of your Planetary Akashic Records with no regrets and nothing left unresolved.

108- Return to Wu Ji Stance / Cosmic Consciousness

As you "Return to Wu Ji Stance", you step into the void and emptiness of Wu Ji, the ultimate, boundless, infinite nature of your authentic Self. You were born from the Essence of Love and Light, and you return to the Essence of your Spirit, which was always accompanying your journey of life. As your energy merges with the Quantum field of All Creation, the 1 of Self fuses with the 8 of eternal motion and change, and the 9 of rebirthing emerges, lifting you into recreating yourself with the 0 of absolute Life force, the spinning of the Macrocosmic Orbit finding its way into the microcosmic atoms of your manifestation. You are One with Source and with All things, beings, stars and beyond, and this enlightened realization unleashes the unconditional love of your essential nature. Heaven and Earth are now aligned within your Humanity, and the alchemy of your Light serves the Greater Good of All That Is, All That Was, and All That Will Ever Be. As you "Return to Wu Ji Stance," you are finally returning "Home".

OUTCOME

As I strive to balance my inner world and outer expression through the discipline of Tai Chi Chuan and Qigong, I have become the disciple of my own life. The Tao Teh Ching states: "He who knows men is clever; He who knows himself has insight. He who conquers men has force; He who conquers himself is truly strong. He who knows when he has got enough is rich; He who stays where he has found his true home endures long, and he who dies but perishes not enjoys real longevity."

I have found "home" and for this I am forever grateful to all my teachers, guides, loved ones and all the brothers and sisters who share the joy of the Tao. You have helped open my consciousness and brought about the realization that Life is a sacred gift, that Love is its essence, and that Spirit is its divine manifestation.

"Heaven is intuition. Connection to Heaven raises us up and exalts us."

Through Heaven we find our mission.

Earth is thought. Connection with Earth connects us with others.

Through Earth, we find a place in the world." Ta Chuan, The Great treatise

TAI CHI CHUAN NAMES/ EXPRESSIONS

SECTION 1/SELF

0- Wu Ji Stance / Creation
1- Tai Chi Commencement / Oneness
2- Ward-Off / Duality
3- Double Ward-Off / Sacred Geometry
4- Roll Back / Overview
5- Press / Limitations
6- Push / Spirit into Matter
7- Single Whip / Past Karma
8- Lift Hands and Step Up / Self-Knowledge
9- White Crane Spreads its Wings / Inner Knowing
10- Brush Knee and Step Forward / Outer Expression
11- Play the Lute / Song of Spirit
12/13/14- Brush Knee and Step Forward /
Awakening the Warrior Within
15- Play the Lute / Call of Spirit
16- Brush Knee and Step Forward / Path of Choice
17- Dragon Step, Forward, Parry and Punch /
Power of Transformation
18- Withdraw and Push / Centering Within
19- Cross Hands / Balance

SECTION 2/ DUALITY

20- Embrace Tiger and Return to the Mountain /
Embracing your Fears
21- Grasp the Sparrow's Tail / Power of the Will

22- Bagua Fish / Emotional Self
23- Fist Under Elbow / Alignment
24/25/26- Step Back and Repulse Monkey / Contemplation
27- Diagonal Flying / Karmic Wheel
28- Lift Hands and Step Up / Spirit Guidance
29- White Crane Spreads its Wings / Self-Realization
30- Brush Knee and Step Forward / Path of Recognition
31- Needle at Sea Bottom / Ocean of Compassion
32- Fan Through Back / Determination
33- Turn Around and Whip Punch / Facing your Shadow
34- Dragon Step, Forward, Parry and Punch /
    Cause and Effect
35- Grasp the Sparrow's tail / Responsibility
36- Single Whip / Self Acceptance
37- Wave Hands like Clouds / The Observer
38- Single Whip / Vision
39- High Pat the Horse / Freedom
40- Separate Right Foot / The Manifester
41- Separate Left Foot / Standing in Duality
42- Turn Around and Kick / Expanding the New Self
43/44- Brush Knee and Step Forward / Emotional Harmony
45- Step Forward and Punch Downward / Courage
46- Turn Around and Whip Punch / Resolution
47- Dragon Step, Forward, Parry and Punch /
    Karmic Retribution
48- Kick with Right Foot / Equilibrium
49- Taming the Tiger Stance / Taming the Fears
50/51- Strike the Tiger Left and Right / Negative Ego
52- Kick with Right Foot / Polarity
53- Double Wind Fills the Ears / Internal Dialogue
54/55- Kick with Left and Right Foot / Self-Reliance
56- Dragon Step Forward, Parry and Punch /
    Healing the Past

SECTION 3/ UNITY

91- Wave Hands like Clouds / Hermit's Journey
92- Single Whip / Commitment
93- High Pat the Horse / Angelic Presence
94- Cross Palms / Crossing Over
95- Turn Around and Kick with Right Foot / Independence
96- Step Forward and Punch Low / Pathways
97- Step Forward and Grasp the Sparrow's Tail / Source
98- Single Whip / Aiming to the Light
99- Snake Creeps Down / Death of Initiation
100- Step Up to Form Seven Stars / Heavenly Bodies
101- Step Back to Ride Tiger / Higher Self
102- Turn Around and Sweep the Lotus / Spiritual Destiny
103- Shoot Tiger with Bow / Holographic Expression
104- Dragon Step, Forward, Parry and Punch / Spiritual Ancestry
105- Withdraw and Push / Path of Mastery
106- Cross Hands / Enlightenment
107- Close Tai Chi / Heaven and Earth
108- Return to Wu Chi Stance / Cosmic Consciousness

BOOKS REFERENCE

- Angeles Arrien "The Fourfold Way"
- Jou, Tsung Hwa "The Tao of Tai-Chi Chuan"
- Ted Andrews "Animal-Speak"
- Lynn Buess "Forever Numerology"

ARTISTS

- Magali Noth- Book cover
- Magali Noth- Animal drawings
- Sifu Fong Ha- Chinese Calligraphy

Printed in the United States
By Bookmasters